SAFAR

A LITERARY JOURNEY THROUGH ARAB CINEMA

– page 122

18. internationales literaturfestival berlin

05 – 15 09 2018

02 09 Sun — BERLIN LIEST

05 09 Wed — OPENING:
IGOR LEVIT [RUS / D]
EVA MENASSE [A / D]
BURGHART KLAUSSNER [D]

06 09 Thu — FRIDA NILSSON [S]
AI WEIWEI [CHN / D]

07 09 Fri — CHARMAINE CRAIG [USA]
MELBA ESCOBAR DE NOGALES [CO]
OLIVIER GUEZ [F]

08 09 Sat — MASANDE NTSHANGA [ZA]
BRUCE PASCOE [AUS]

09 09 Sun — SCOTT ANDERSON [USA]
MARÍA CECILIA BARBETTA [RA / D]

10 09 Mon — SYDNEY SMITH [CDN]

11 09 Tue — JULI ZEH [D]

12 09 Wed — ZAZA BURCHULADZE [GE]
PRABDA YOON [T]

13 09 Thu — DAVID GRAEBER [GB]

14 09 Fri — DIDIER ERIBON [F]
MICHAEL ONDAATJE [CDN]
BERNHARD SCHLINK [D]

15 09 Sat — JENNIFER EGAN [USA]
MAJA LUNDE [N]
NIGEL SLATER [GB]

06 – 09 09
POETRY NIGHTS

07 – 09 09
DECOLONIZING WOR(L)DS

09 09
GRAPHIC NOVEL DAY

ART OF COOKING
THE EVOLUTION OF HUMAN CULTURE
NATURE WRITING
POLITICS OF DRUGS
REFUGEES WORLDWIDE

www.literaturfestival.com

ADVANCE NOTICE

The 2018 Lecture

of the Saif Ghobash Banipal Prize for Arabic Literary Translation

7pm, Friday 9 November 2018

The Knowledge Centre, British Library
96 Euston Road, London NW1 2DB

Guest speaker

Adonis

Photo: Bahget Iskander

Is this the time of translation? And is translation a second act of creation?

In the lecture Adonis will consider the relationship of translation to human identity and explore the fact that human beings live in the same chronological moment, but in multiple, disparate moments culturally. And in the translation of poetry, the responsibility of the translator is to breathe new life into the linguistic destruction that is the translated poem – the migrant living in an alien house.

Adonis is an internationally renowned poet, essayist, philosopher and theoretician of Arab poetics. Referred to in interviews as "the greatest living poet of the Arab world", this "grand old man of poetry, secularism and free speech in the Arab world" has been writing poetry for 75 years and has more than fifty published works in Arabic of poetry, criticism, essays, and translations. His modernist influence on Arabic poetry is often compared to that of T S Eliot on Anglophone poetry.

Banipal Trust for Arab Literature, 1 Gough Square, London EC4A 3DE
Email: info@banipaltrust.org.uk Web: www.banipaltrust.org.uk

Sheikh Hamad Award for Translation and International Understanding (SHATIU) is accepting nominations for the year 2018 in the following categories:

1. Translation from Arabic into English	(200,000 USD)
2. Translation from English into Arabic	(200,000 USD)
3. Translation from Arabic into German	(200,000 USD)
4. Translation from German into Arabic	(200,000 USD)
5. Achievement Award	(200,000 USD)

SHATIU is also accepting nominations for **achievement awards** in translation from and into the following languages:

Translation from Arabic into Bosnian	(100,000 USD)
Translation from Bosnian into Arabic	(100,000 USD)
Translation from Arabic into Italian	(100,000 USD)
Translation from Italian into Arabic	(100,000 USD)
Translation from Arabic into Japanese	(100,000 USD)
Translation from Japanese into Arabic	(100,000 USD)
Translation from Arabic into Russian	(100,000 USD)
Translation from Russian into Arabic	(100,000 USD)
Translation from Arabic into Swahili	(100,000 USD)
Translation from Swahili into Arabic	(100,000 USD)

Deadline for submissions is August 31/2018

Please visit our website **www.hta.qa/en** for information about the Award, rules of submission and nomination forms.

   HamadTAward Phone: (+974) 66570349 Email: info@hta.qa

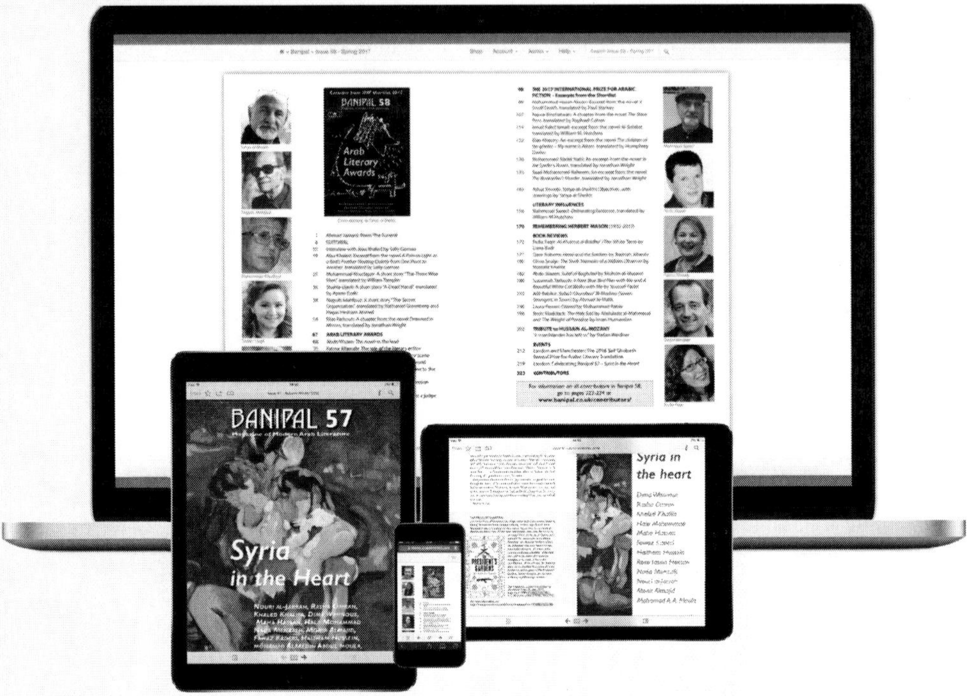

BANIPAL

Magazine of Modern Arab Literature

Banipal magazine, founded in 1998, takes its name from Ashurbanipal (668–627 BC), the last great king of Assyria and patron of the arts, whose outstanding achievement was to assemble in his capital Nineveh, Mesopotamia, from all over his empire, the first systematically organised library in the ancient Middle East. The thousands of clay tablets of Sumerian, Babylonian and Assyrian writings included the famous Mesopotamian epics of the Creation, the Flood, and Gilgamesh, many folk tales, fables, proverbs, prayers and omen texts.

Source: *Encyclopaedia Britannica*

PUBLISHER: Margaret Obank

EDITOR: Samuel Shimon

ADDITIONAL TRANSLATION: Adil Babikir, Jonathan Wright, Nancy Roberts, Ghada Mourad, Marthe Nelissen

COVER ARTWORK: Lara Arafeh

LAYOUT: Banipal Publishing

WEBSITE: www.banipal.co.uk

EDITOR: editor@banipal.co.uk

PUBLISHER: margaret@banipal.co.uk

INQUIRIES: info@banipal.co.uk

SUBSCRIPTIONS: subscribe@banipal.co.uk

ADDRESS: 1 Gough Square, London EC4A 3DE

PRINTED BY Marston Book Services
Milton Park, Abingdon OX14 4SB

Photographs not accredited have been donated, photographers unknown.

BANIPAL 62 – A Literary Journey through Arab Cinema

This issue is ISBN 978-0-9956369-6-5. RRP £10, €12, USD15

BANIPAL, ISSN 1461-5363, is published three times a year by Banipal Publishing, 1 Gough Square, London EC4A 3DE

www.banipal.co.uk

Azouz Begag

Lutfiya al-Dulaimi

Ahmad Ali El-Zein

Abdelrashid Mahmoudi

Liana Badr

L'OPIUM
ET LE
BATON

Un film de Youssef Chahine
Le Sixième Jour
DALIDA
Mohsen Mohieddine

LES
CHEVAUX
DE DIEU

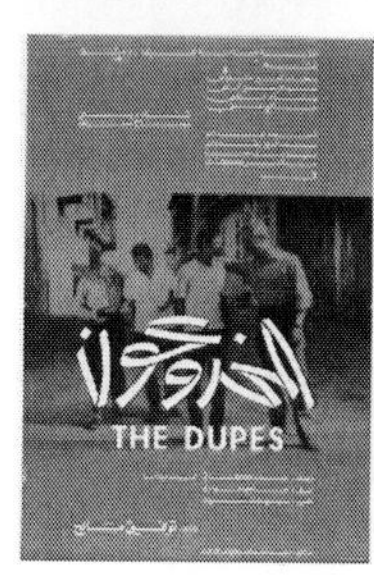
THE DUPES

Saif Ghobash Banipal Prize for Arabic Literary Translation

Nominations for the 2018 Prize

In the thirteenth year of the prize there are 20 entries, comprising two collections of poetry and eighteen novels including one graphic novel. The entries are listed by title in alphabetical order of translator.

JUDGING PANEL

The judges this year are editor and translator Georgia de Chamberet, publisher and editor Pete Ayrton, novelist Fadia Faqir, and lecturer in philosophical theology and translator Sophia Vasalou.

THE ENTRIES

In Jerusalem and Other Poems by Tamim al-Barghouti, translated by Radwa Ashour, Ahdaf Soueif, Tamim al-Barghouti, (Interlink Books)

No Road to Paradise by Hassan Daoud, translated by Marilyn Booth (Hoopoe Fiction, AUC) Press)

Divine Names by Luay Abdul-Ilah, translated by Judy Cumberbatch (Mira Publishing)

Hend and the Soldiers by Badriah Albeshr, translated by Sanna Dhahir (CMES Pubs, Univ Texas at Austin)

The American Quarter by Jabbour Donahy, translated by Paula Haydar (Interlink Books)

The Apartment in Bab el-Louk by Donia Maher (with illustrations by Ganzeer and Ahmad Nady), translated by Elisabeth Jaquette (Darf Publishers)

Suslov's Daughter by Habib Abdulrab Sarori, translated by Elisabeth Jaquette (Darf Publishers)

Using Life by Ahmed Naji, translated by Ben Koerber (CMES Publications, University of Texas at Austin)

The President's Gardens by Muhsin Al-Ramli, translated by Luke Leafgren (MacLehose Press)

Concerto al-Quds by Adonis, translated by Khaled Mattawa (Yale University Press)

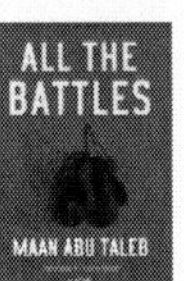

Tales of Yusuf Tadrus by Adel Esmat, translated by Mandy McClure (AUC Press)

All The Battles by Maan Abu Taleb, translated by Robin Moger (Hoopoe Fiction, AUC Press)

Embrace on Brooklyn Bridge by Ezzedine C. Fishere, translated by John Peate (Hoopoe Fiction, AUC Press)

Gaza Weddings by Ibrahim Nasrallah, translated by Nancy Roberts (Hoopoe Fiction, AUC Press)

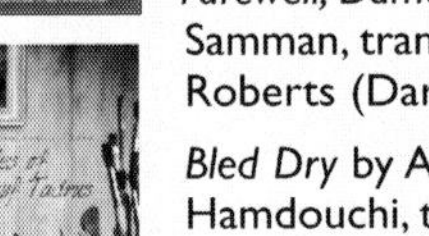

Farewell, Damascus by Ghada Samman, translated by Nancy Roberts (Darf Publishers)

Bled Dry by Abdelilah Hamdouchi, translated by Benjamin Smith (Hoopoe Fiction, AUC Press)

The Blueness of the Evening: Selected Poems of Hassan Najmi by Hassan Najmi, translated by Mbarek Sryfi and Eric Sellin (University of Arkansas Press)

Fractured Destinies by Rabai Al-Madhoun, translated by Paul Starkey (Hoopoe Fiction, AUC Press)

The Baghdad Eucharist by Sinan Antoon, translated by Maia Tabet (Hoopoe Fiction, AUC Press)

Frankenstein in Baghdad by Ahmed Saadawi, translated by Jonathan Wright (Oneworld)

The **Shortlist** will be announced in December, and the **Winner** at the end of January 2019. The **Award Ceremony**, hosted by the Society of Authors, will take place February/March 2019.

The prize is administered for the Banipal Trust for Arab Literature by the Society of Authors

EDITORIAL

This summer Banipal welcomes two wonderful collaborations – with the 40th year of the Assilah Festival in Morocco, and with the Arab British Centre's SAFAR Film Festival.

The Assilah Festival is very close to our hearts – an international and inspirational meeting point every year for dialogue, discovery and creativity, with arts and culture at its centre. As part of our collaboration with the 40th Festival we present testimonies by international figures who have participated in the Festival over the years – and some memories of our own visits.

The theme of the fourth SAFAR Film Festival is "A Literary Journey through Arab Cinema". In our 66-page feature we include introductions to the festival by the Centre's director Nadia El-Sebai, and the festival's curator Joseph Fahim, nine articles which each considers a particular book and film pair. There's an interview with Daoud Abdel Sayed, director of the famous Egyptian film *Kit Kat*, an important call for more women writers to have film adaptations by Haitham El-Zobaidi, and a presentation by award-winning filmmaker and photographer Koutaiba al-Janabi of his latest film, *Stories of Passers Through*.

Banipal 62 continues our policy, started this year, of supplementing excerpts of novels with synopses, reviews, portraits or critical appraisal of the entire works so that the reader can enjoy deeper dialogue and understanding. The opening work is from a novel by Iraqi author Lutfiya al-Dulaimi that plays through a panorama of Iraqi history from the early 20th century to the present day in a family saga, and is accompanied by a fascinating portrait of her writings by Iraqi critic and poet Ali Abdulameer Ejam. We were pleased to receive a number of complimentary reactions to this new presentation style from readers of *Banipal 61*. Other major authors included in this issue are Ahmad Ali El-Zein, Azouz Begag and Abdelrashid Mahmoudi.

The Literary Influences column features a moving account by Palestinian author Liana Badr, who will be well-known to Anglophone readers through her translated works, of her passion for reading from a very early age.

We report on this year's Arab literary awards – The Sheikh Zayed Book Award and the International Prize for Arabic Fiction – augmented by Ahmed Saadawi's novel *Frankenstein in Baghdad* being shortlisted for the 2018 Man Booker International Prize, and are pleased to see literary awards being promoting in the magazine's pages. However, we cannot mention these without mentioning our own Saif Ghobash Banipal Prize for Arabic Literary Translation, whose nominations for the 2018 prize are revealed on the previous page.

We are also thrilled to give advance notice (on page 3) of the Saif Ghobash Banipal Prize annual lecture, which, on 9 November at the British Library, will be given by Adonis, the internationally renowned Syrian poet and "grand old man of poetry, secularism and free speech in the Arab world".

LUTFIYA AL-DULAIMI

The Journal of Subhi al-Kutubkhani

EXCERPTS FROM THE NOVEL
LOVERS, A PHONOGRAPH AND TIMES

TRANSLATED BY NANCY ROBERTS

"We all know that art is not truth.
Art is a lie that makes us realize truth."
– Pablo Picasso[1]

Nuha opened the first volume of her great-grandfather's journal, and found the following quote written out in beautiful Persian script:

We were born out of love.
We were created out of love.
We are drawn to love.
Indeed, we are being held in love's arms.

The Grand Sheikh, the Sultan of Gnostics,
Muhyi ad-Din Ibn Arabi

When she turned the page, she found a yellowed, folded-up piece of paper containing the name 'Subhi al-Kutubkhani' written in various kinds of Arabic script: Persian, Kufic, Thuluth, and Diwani. Examining the aging piece of paper, she found the calligrapher's name – Saad or Asaad – at the bottom. She especially liked her great-grandfather's name written in the Diwani script with its graceful,

sweeping curves. It made her think of musical phrase marks. Enchanted by the various types of script, she could hear the letters singing – rustling like the leaves of a tree being washed by the rain. Every letter contained a hidden spirit, every dot a mystery, and every curve, a subtle allusion to another time or realm.

"It seems our ancestor Subhi had refined taste," she mused aloud. "He was a connoisseur of calligraphy and art."

She carefully folded up the little piece of paper and, with a mixture of dread and curiosity, made up her mind to read everything that her great-grandfather had recorded in these yellowed tomes with his plume pen and black Chinese ink. As she read, she discovered that he would at times conceal his identity by talking about himself in the third person, as though he were somebody who had lived with him and observed him and his closest companions, while at other times

Lovers, a Phonograph and Times, presents an account of Iraq's development from the early twentieth century under Ottoman rule through to the century's end and the post-US-occupation era. A composite fabric of historical, anthropological and societal detail is woven together through the novel's narrative by the unearthing of important information about four successive generations of the Kutubkhani family.

The novel relies on a narrative pattern that might be described as "modernist classicalism", a description that has come to characterize the contemporary novel in the post-Modern period, with its fantastical ploys, thereby rendering the novel a medium capable of conveying to readers a vast, kaleidoscopic store of knowledge. As such, the novel has become a serious competitor to historical, societal and political theses that reveal the various contexts which go to make up Iraq's identity, as well as the influences that have cast their shadows over individuals' lives and left their distinctive imprint on Iraqi place and time.

In its overall form, the novel adopts a non-linear approach to time by juxtaposing the life of Nuha al-Kutubkhani and her subsequent evolution with that of her grandfather, Subhi al-Kutubkhani by way of his memoirs. This juxtaposition brings to light numerous details that are key to an understanding of the Iraqi situation against its historical, political and societal background. The novel is likewise replete with scientific and cultural data that provide a panoramic view of the past century of Iraq's history – a century charged with societal, political and individual upheavals reflected vividly in the extensions, transformations and transitions of the Kutubkhani family.

he wrote in his own voice. In a brief preface of just a few lines, he had explained what he intended to do, saying:

> I, Subhi al-Kutubkhani, am confessing to these notebooks, which now bear the burdens of my years. I shall reveal myself, my passions, and the bitterness of my soul. I shall put myself on trial, hold myself to account.

He then launched into the content of his memoir:

> And now to our topic: I'm alone, holed up in the tea storage room, immersed in the scents of tea from India, Ceylon and China . . . I can hear the cooing of the pigeons in the bitter orange trees, and perhaps in the date palms as well. I've been alone ever since I was a boy. I didn't play with my brothers and sisters. In fact, I had no interest in playing. Even now, I'm still alone in this house. I tremble with grief, and ask my heart: "What will I do with my life amidst this stifling world and all my failures?" Even though I'm surrounded by my family in my own home town, I'm a stranger, an alien. What disaffection the spirit must endure when its loneliness becomes a never-ending fate! I'm divorced from everything around me. Like an exotic plant in a cactus field, I've rejected the customs and traditions that have been imposed on me.
>
> I weep in regret over my spirit. I weep for my mother, my sisters and brothers, the guards, the immortalized nanny Umm Nu'man, and for all the people who are content with the inherited slavery in which they find themselves.
>
> What I write has nothing to do with the recording of history and events in the country. Rather, I'm writing about people's spiritual suffering, their stifled longings. I write about people's dreams, their sins, and the madness of the heart. What's written in my diaries about events and facts – which I see only from the outside – is nothing but a wooden frame for fogged-up mirrors like the old oval-shaped one in my sister Wafiqa's room.
>
> The facts I gather have been erased anyway. There's nothing real about history and its recorded events. What's real is the fact that we're deceived by so many things. As for the events taking place all over the country, they're the stuff of intimida-

tion and exaggeration. The writing of history is a deceptive, misleading manoeuvre. People see events from a single side, dictated by their whims and desires. They write about them from whichever angle suits their inclinations, their sense of identity, their interests, their cruel designs. There's nothing real in the world but the alienation of the spirit, love stories, loss, and the debilitating longing to rest in a time and place that are safe from harm. All that remains is but the deceptive games of sorcerers, the work of highway robbers, and the cruelty of those who strike people's necks with the sword.

(This is what I wrote before travelling to Istanbul.)

. . . And now to our topic again.

I'm penning these lines after years and years of living. I've experienced life in its most splendorous forms. I've lived abroad, I've known hardship and privation, passionate love, self-denial, and adventure. Some times I've risen, and at others I've sunk to the depths of misery. Then I've put my life in order again after years of seeing things fall apart. According to what my father recorded in our family register, I was born in Baghdad in 1887 AD. But from the time I was a young child and then into adolescence, I saw that I myself was different from the closed society around me. It was a hopeless world steeped in superstition, greed and sin. I became a resentful, isolated, wayward son with a troubled heart and a suspicious mind.

I'll let my writings speak for me, sometimes in someone else's voice, and sometimes in my own. All I ask of those who read my memoirs is to think deeply about what I've written. My hope is that they'll find some benefit in an old dusty book as they observe what's happened to me – and to us – over the course of our lives.

And now to our topic . . .

I, Subhi al-Kutubkhani, was being buffeted back and forth between overwhelming desires, the murmurings of the spirit, the sexual urges of my youth, and my rage over the conditions that prevailed in the Baghdad vilayet. It was governed at the time by Namiq Pasha the Younger, who'd been appointed by Sultan

> Abdulhamid. I spent my nights and days immersed in clamorous dreams. I would wake up every morning intoxicated from the events I'd witnessed and the pleasures I'd known. I would then hurry to set them down in writing in a big gilded volume bound in black leather. Whenever I wrote down a dream, I would relive the ecstasy I'd experienced in the dream by imagining it all over again. I know how difficult it is to describe ecstasy. So how could I write about the tremors of delight, and pleasure's nectar in the mouth? How could I describe the sweet purl that raced through my veins until I fell unconscious? How can anyone record the taste of ecstasy and the flavour of pleasures? There were no words to describe all the outpourings from my visions and the desires of my deprived youth. Yet, oblivious to this fact, I just went on writing down my visions of delight with Chinese black ink in the white book of dreams . . .

Nuha closed the first volume. Inside it she had found some loose papers that bore an earlier date. The handwriting on some of the pages was sloppy, while on others it was so faint you could hardly read it. There were also entire lines that had been crossed out.

"Have you looked at these?" Nuha asked her father.

"Yes. But I couldn't make out the handwriting, so I'm leaving them to you! I haven't got the patience to dig through it all and read the bits that are so faint."

"I'll try rewriting them. But first I need time to read through them carefully."

"You've got all the time you need."

A couple of days later, Nuha brought her father a number of pages that she'd typed out on the computer.

"This is what I've managed to rewrite out of forty pages of material. The pages are tattered, and some of the lines are all blurry. They're about your grandfather Subhi's years as a young man, his trip to Istanbul to study there, and his sister Wafiqa. Would you like me to read you what I've gathered from the material so far?"

"No, that's all right. Leave it here and I'll read it when I've got a quiet moment."

"When will we open the other chest?"

"Everything in its time."

"Here they are, then. I'm going to work on the other bundle of papers now. They have to do with his childhood and adolescence, so they're earlier than the events we read about in the bound volume."

* * *

Desires of the Heart

"O my soul, do not aspire to immortal life,
but exhaust the limits of the possible."
– Pindar, from his ode, *Pythian 3*

Nothing can change the mysterious courses of Fate: neither tears, nor the resistance of the spirit, nor the sorrows of the heart. In Baghdad, you're surprised by news both bad and good. You're surprised by disasters as much as you are by happy events, and they carry you beyond expectations. You see golden stars raining down light, and clouds forming a spectrum of colourful waves or dusk-hued hills in enchanted skies. Nothing is as possible as the wonders that we could never have anticipated, the kinds of things no set of probabilities would remotely support. Out of the blue, Nuha got a phone call from her aunt Hana, informing her of an appointment she would never have thought possible with the insular, mystically inclined Professor Nadir, who had a special interest in making odd gadgets out of old machine parts and the like. His sister Manal said his room was lined with chalkboards on which he wrote out the symbols for his cosmological formulas and his ideas related to advanced mathematics and physics. Nuha and her aunt would be going to see him about their broken phonograph. They hoped he might be able to make a replacement arm to hold its needle so that they could recover some of her ancestors' secrets, recorded on abandoned phonograph records they'd come across.

After discovering the despicable pettiness of the world through the war he'd waged after graduating from university, Nadir An-Niya had withdrawn from public life. His harrowing experience was like a concave mirror that accentuated people's ugliness and aggressive tendencies, revealing the worst in the human soul. After teaching for several years, he'd become increasingly aware of how disfigured and misshapen people's psyches can be, and how aggressively inclined. He'd also seen how similar the distortions people exhibit can be despite the dissimilarity in their causes. He resigned from his job without hesitation or regret, since it was obvious to him that the country was falling apart, and its schools collapsing. The educational system was in decline with curricula based on obsolete notions, leaving teachers and university professors without ability to impact on the character formation of their students, to bring out their gifts and talents, or identify those with innovative minds. In fact, these people didn't even want to appear to be influencing the events afflicting society, which was divided over the meaning of past events, and riddled with conflicting factions and ethnic groups. Consequently, he had isolated himself from the outside world, content to relate to it from a distance via his metaphysical perceptions, or his computer screen. As far as he was concerned, the world was a deformed, leprous creature to be avoided at all costs. It was enough for people just to endure their unspoken sense of ignominy in the face of this vicious planet. Everybody on earth was being degraded and humiliated, and this realization would be enough to prevent anybody from enjoying life's pleasures, feeling at peace with life, and savouring the gifts of beauty that they deserved.

Nadir couldn't sleep at night from thinking about all the human sacrifices being offered up day and night on the altar of doctrines and policies. Sometimes he even closed himself off from his small circle of close friends, immersing himself for hours in readings on the cosmos, the philosophy of knowledge, and the latest developments in physics, especially quantum and subatomic physics. It was his way of distancing himself for some time from a world being devoured by people's stupidity and greed. For the most part he ignored the passage of time, preferring to deal with the concepts of time and space in the abstract, which had a way of cheering him up and lightening the mental and emotional burdens that come from thinking about day-to-day affairs and ever-changing circumstances. It pained him to see how people's temperaments were being transmuted into something he didn't even recognize, immersed in oneupmanship and fierce competition like ravenous beasts fighting over fresh prey.

When his sister Manal told him that a guest would be coming to ask for his help with something, Nadir neither welcomed the idea nor rejected it. The blank expression on his face suggested nothing in particular. He crossed the living room without another word, and headed upstairs to his room.

"So will you meet with her?" Manal asked impatiently, anxious to know whether to confirm the appointment or not. He made no reply.

"Nadir!" she called out again. "Are you going to meet with our guest, or not??"

"Maybe," he answered from his room. "I don't know, actually."

After typing up some new entries from her great-grandfather's journal about his family and his marriage and changes that had taken place in Baghdad in 1908, Nuha gave the typed version to her father, who was anxiously awaiting these exciting chapters of his forebear's diary. She made him a cup of hot tea and opened the window in his room that overlooked beds of lilies and roses, bougainvillea bushes whose fiery red blossoms lit up the outdoors, and a small fountain where sparrows bathed and hopped about, their fluttering wings sending out sprinklings of water as they took to flight again.

Nuha put on a pair of dark blue jeans, and a blouse decorated with tiny colourful flowers against a white background. Then she tied her long hair behind her neck, and sat down to wait for her Aunt Hana, who was planning to accompany her to her much-anticipated destination. Hana announced her arrival with her usual racket. She honked in a special rhythm that Nuha recognised right away: toot to-toot tooooot! Then she got out of her car and rang the doorbell over and over as though she'd been waiting all day. And as if that weren't enough, she called through the door: "Nuha! Nuha! Come on now, hurry up!"

Nuha came out and gave her aunt a hug, and they drove off.

"We're going to my friend Manal's house," Hana explained. "I'll introduce you to her and to her brother, Professor Nadir. Some time back their older sister emigrated with her husband to Canada, and their brother, a doctor, went as a refugee to Germany. Then their father passed away, and they've lived by themselves ever since. They were both offered immigrant visas, but they turned them down. Manal didn't want to leave her job at the Ministry of Agriculture, and Nadir's determined never to uproot himself from Iraq. He says he could never survive away from home, even if staying there means terror, fear, isolation, and always expecting the worst!

"By the way, I'm going to drop you off at their house and go on to the dentist's. I've got an appointment and I don't want to be late. When I'm finished I'll come back to join you. But just so you know:

Nadir might not be willing to see you, with or without good reason! But don't be discouraged. His sister Manal told me that if it didn't work out today, he might agree to meet with you some other day when he's in the mood for conversing with strangers."

It was mid-afternoon when the two women arrived. They got out of the car and went up to the house, and Hana rang the doorbell. Fragrant breezes were wafting out of the garden, strains of music were stealing out through one of the windows, and the delicious aroma of pies informed them that Manal was at work in her kitchen. A few moments later, the door opened and Manal peered out with her thin frame, her glossy red hair, and her barely perceptible smile.

"Hello, Nuha," she said. "We meet at last! I haven't seen you since you were in high school. How pretty you've gotten!"

Nuha blushed at the unexpected compliment and gave a bashful smile.

"Come on in," Manal said.

"I'll be leaving Nuha here," Hana announced. "I've got to get to a dentist's appointment."

"As usual!" Manal remarked wryly. "Conflicting appointments, and excuses galore!"

"I'll be back in around an hour and have coffee with you."

Manal accompanied her guest to the parlour, where they chatted for a while about the latest news, including the explosions, power cuts, and the flood that had inundated parts of Baghdad. Then Manal excused herself to make the coffee and inform Nadir of Nuha's arrival.

Nuha settled into her chair, holding the broken phonograph arm in a thick plastic bag. Glancing around the room, she glimpsed a bookcase filled with books and got up to take a closer look at them. It gave her a kind of satisfaction and joy to see that the collection included books she'd read and loved: *The Mysterious Universe* by Sir James Jeans, *A Brief History of Time* by Stephen Hawking, and *The Evolution of Physics* by Albert Einstein. She also glimpsed works she adored by Ibn Arabi, Farid ad-Din al-Attar, Shihab ad-Din as-Suhrawardi, and the novels of Dostoevsky, Herman Hesse, and Thomas Mann. There were a couple of abstract oil paintings on the opposite wall, and atop the glass table in the centre of the room glistened tiny crystal figurines in assorted animal shapes: giraffes, whales, bears, birds and seals. At the end of the table there was a transparent flower vase containing a bouquet of orange lilies nestled between spear-like green leaves.

Just then Nuha heard Manal calling her brother: "Nadir! Aren't you going to come down? Our guest's here. Come and have some coffee with us."

From upstairs she heard a man's voice say: "I'm coming."

Once he'd made it down the stairs, he extended his hand to Nuha, who was still standing in front of the bookcase.

"Nadir," he said in introduction.

"Nuha al-Kutubkhani," she returned.

Then Nuha went pale and said nothing more. Nadir's features reminded her of the man she'd seen so many times before in fleeting visions and dreams. His expression had changed a bit by now, but when she took a long look at him, he recovered his original appearance. Was this really happening? Could the man of her visions take shape before her as a living being?

Nuha stood there motionless, surprised stiff, and engrossed in her tumultuous thoughts. She'd been so flustered by the resemblance between Nadir and the man she'd conjured in her imagination that she wasn't quite sure how to engage him in conversation. She gaped at the person standing before her. His inscrutable way of looking at her gave her the impression that he was mentally absent. He seemed to look at her without actually looking, which was just the opposite of the man in her visions, who pierced her with his clear, direct gaze. She concluded that Nadir must be the prudish, rigid sort. Even so, she decided to summon the courage to talk to him.

"You've got quite a library, Professor Nadir," she began. "It includes classics on Sufism, physics, mathematics, and music. They're all subjects I'm interested in, and I consider them extremely important for people living in this day and age. In fact, they're important no matter what age you live in."

"Yes, they really are extremely important," Nadir concurred, "to me, at least!"

He invited her to sit down, and she took her place on the large sofa, which was upholstered in dark brown velvet and strewn with colourful silk cushions.

"It's an honour to meet you, Professor Nadir. I really appreciate your giving me some of your precious time. My Aunt Hana's told me amazing things about you."

"Well, Miss Hana tends to exaggerate a bit. There's nothing amazing about me, actually. And my time isn't as precious as you might imagine. Either way, time's passing. Sometimes we try to fill it with ideas or actions, or we do useless things as if we were here only to play. Life's nothing but a game, after all. It's a fact that's lost on a lot of people, who seem to treat it with the utmost seriousness. By the way, according to game theory, everything we do in this life has a precise mathematical model associated with it."

"I've never heard of game theory before."

"If you're interested, I can give you a copy of *Theory of Games and Economic Behaviour* by John von Neumann and Oskar Morgenstern. It will familiarize you with its fundamental principles. Don't worry about the technical details or the formulas. Just focus on the ideas and concepts."

"Thanks – I'd like that. I hear you're interested in old phonograph players, especially Edison's version. That's why I asked to meet you, actually. So what's the secret behind this fascination of yours?"

"I've got the latest model, the kind that plays discs. I've actually never got ahold of an Edison-style phonograph, even though I've looked all over for one. As for how I got interested in these machines, it goes back to the connection between the appearance of the phonograph player and an important phase in the evolution of physics. Around the time when the phonograph was first being manufactured and people were starting to record sounds on it, Einstein announced the theory of relativity. In those days, people dreamed of capturing the voices of the greats who had departed, the idea being that sound is an indestructible form of energy. Numerous attempts were made after that, but without any definitive outcomes."

"Why were they so interested in the voices of the greats?"

"It seems they just wanted to confirm certain perceptions about them."

"Did you ever try to record any of them yourself?"

"No, I never did. My main interest was in mechanics and music, even when I was a student in the Faculty of Sciences."

"You were in the Faculty of Sciences? Did you ever meet my brother Walid? He was in the Geology Department, and had started writing his Master's dissertation, but his circumstances took an unexpected turn, and he ended up emigrating from Iraq."

"Unfortunately, I never did. Maybe he came to the faculty after I did."

"I was wondering, just out of curiosity: why did you study physics in a country that doesn't appreciate science and scientists? What did you expect? Did you choose physics because of the grades you got in your final exams at secondary school?"

"Actually, I scored nearly 100 percent, which would have been high enough for me to go into medicine if I'd wanted to. I got the second highest mark in Iraq that year. But I decided to go into the Faculty of Sciences because I loved physics too much to give it up."

"So did you go into applied physics?"

"No, actually. I went into theoretical physics, because it's closer to the world of ideas. I like symbols, and I can't stand excessive talk, rhetorical language and all the other chit-chat that floods our lives now. It pours out of the mouths of people on television screens who don't appreciate the value of time and nearly suffocates us. As for mathematics, it's my other, 'parallel', passion, you might say, because it reduces the world for us into discrete symbols in a way which I find absolutely incredible."

"So it seems I'm a really bad guesser!"

"Not really. It's just that I'm really unpredictable. Don't forget, I'm also interested in making weird gadgets, even though I'm more concerned with ideas themselves than I am with applying them. It's not your fault I'm such a contradiction!"

"We've all got things about us that don't make sense."

"So what are your interests?"

"Currently, my dad's got me pouring over my great-grandfather's journal entries and typing them up for him. That's my only job right now. I read books. I listen to music. But all in all, it's a useless life."

"And what, in your opinion, would a 'useful' life look like? Is it essential that one produce visible results? As a matter of fact, you're achieving two things of benefit at present: your father's happiness, and the personal enjoyment you're getting out of discovering the contents of this journal."

"And is that enough?"

"One lesson I've learned in life is not to ask for the impossible. As the Greek poet Pindar once said: 'O my soul, do not aspire to immortal life, but exhaust the limits of the possible.'"

"In this country, even the simplest things have become impossibilities. How ironic: I strove for the impossible, and lost even the possible."

"You're right. Our life here isn't a healthy human existence."

Manal served the coffee, whose warm aroma filled the room. Energized by the delicious fragrance, Nuha suddenly noticed that she hadn't felt the time passing during her rambling conversation with Nadir. As she picked up the pink embossed coffee cup, Manal presented her with a plate of chocolate-covered hazelnuts. She took one and munched on it with relish.

"It's so good to see you, Nuha. If it weren't for that broken phonograph, we wouldn't have met!"

"Thank you, Manal. I suppose you've heard that my brother Walid has left the country. So now I've got an even bigger responsibility to take care of my mum and dad."

"Yes, Hana told me he'd got married and adopted a baby, and that he and his new bride had left the country. But that doesn't mean you can't go places once in a while. Don't shut yourself up like my brother Nadir. Get out and live your life!"

"What life is there to live here, Manal?"

"We're governed by our surroundings," Nadir interjected. "We aren't really free. We're being held hostage to circumstances that have been imposed on us. Isolation may not be the ideal choice, but it's a kind of shield that protects us, even from ourselves. It's a defence mechanism devised by our minds to preserve our remaining store of vital energy, and to keep us from wasting it on the useless and mundane. You might be surprised if I told you that the question of inevitability over free will, which used to be confined to circles of classical philosophers, is now being taken up by physics researchers."

Seeing how engaged Nadir was with Nuha, Manal thought to herself: *I haven't see him so open with anybody for a long time!*

"Thank you, Manal," Nuha said as she finished her coffee. "You've been so gracious and hospitable!"

Nadir was sipping the last of his coffee and staring into space when Nuha said: "Professor Nadir, I hope I'm not imposing on you with my request! But this is an arm from a 1902 Edison phonograph that belonged to my great-grandfather. We've got some original cylinders at home, the old kind that was wrapped in tinfoil, but we need to get the arm repaired first and have a needle attached to it before we can find out what's recorded on them. We found some other wax-covered cylinders too, but they're too damaged to be of any use."

"May I ask you a question?"

"Be my guest."

"Why this interest in your family's past?"

"I asked my dad the very same question at first. I couldn't see why he would be so interested in his grandfather's memoirs. But as I worked on them myself, I saw their importance as mirrors of societal conditions in his day, and I started enjoying them the way I would a novel or a film. I'm not a writer and I don't aspire to be one, but I see how a biography or memoir can reveal unexpected things about people's psychological and emotional states, their longings and dreams, and in that way it can help us piece together their life stories."

"Even so, I see spending time poring over old journal entries as a way of frittering away one's life."

"In that case, I think we have a difference of opinion. Our lives may not be easy. But having a project to work on, regardless of how important or unimportant it is, can be a kind of tranquilizer or pain killer that relieves our suffering and alleviates our sense of emptiness."

"So then," Nadir suggested sardonically, "I might write a memoir too, as a way of preserving whatever share I have of a truncated life!"

"Why not? Anybody can write down what he's been through in life. But I personally don't plan to do it. My experience is limited, and it's not much different from what many women of my generation have been through. So I don't think it would be of any value."

"Every event in our lives has some value," Nadir offered.

He examined the broken phonograph arm, turning it over in his hands. After a silence he said, "I might have to look for some tools to help me breathe new life into this thing."

"I don't mean to trouble you."

"On the contrary. It's a treat for me to work on this machine. I'd never imagined that anybody around here had one of these."

"I'm going to be making you awfully busy – sorry about that!"

"But you won't be making me too busy. You'll just be protecting me from the temptation of the door. You see that door over there?"

"Yes . . ."

"Well, it calls out to me. Every morning I hear it inviting me to walk through it. The door is the portal to our destinies. Surprises lie beyond it. On one hand, there might be nothing at all out there. On the other hand, questions might come raining down on me the minute I step outside. I might walk into some ordeal. I might be propelled toward a frightening unknown, and panic at the sight of what's happened to people and to the city. This is the kind of thing I've thought to myself, at least. But now I'm discovering that the door has gifts to offer that I hadn't anticipated."

"So have you been expecting something?"

"Can we live without expectations? The minute I saw you standing there looking at my books, I knew something in my world was going to change."

Nuha was flustered at his unforeseen declaration. No one would ever have expected such a thing to be said at that moment. Troubled, she thought about what to say. Had this hermit-like man picked up on some womanly secret of hers? Had he perceived the inner dimensions of her thoughts, and the longings of her wary spirit? And how was she supposed to respond now that she'd been so thoroughly embarrassed?

With a smile on her face that lit up her eyes, she said: "Am I entitled to be proud of myself for that?"

"You'll regret it if you don't!"

She was surprised all over again by his cryptic reply: "You'll regret it if you don't." It was a loaded statement, open to a variety of interpretations. What exactly was it that she would regret not doing? Would she regret not having been proud of herself for changing something in him? Or having wasted the opportunity to connect with him?

She looked over and saw him holding the phonograph arm, his head bowed. She eyed him with a covert affection. She felt as though she had known him for a thousand years. His features bore a powerful resemblance to those of the man who had enchanted her in the vision. It was as though she recognized those sorrowful eyes, those pursed lips, that broad forehead, and the distracted look that made him all the more mysterious and inaccessible. She knew those nervous hands and their delicate fingers. She was pleased by the fact that she'd been able to anticipate his tone of voice before he spoke to her, thereby confirming her intuition. At that moment she felt herself

The statue in Baghdad of the great poet Abu Nuwas (756–814 CE)

blossoming like a tree in early spring. Then a gust of wind blew her down, leaving her at a rugged crossroads, and she knew she had to make a firm choice as to which fork she would take. Once again she wondered whether the man in her vision had taken on flesh in the form of Nadir.

She thought to herself: *How we complicate our own lives, and turn them into nightmares! Why don't we just say outright what's going on inside us? Why all this hiding behind masks? Why don't I confess to him that he's been occupying my visions?*

"I'll ask a friend of mine about a craftsman we know." said Nadir. "We'll see if he can make us a metal arm like this one."

"So then," she replied, "it looks as though you're going to be going out that door after all!"

"Yep! I'm going to give in to the temptation. Do you believe it?"

"Yes, I believe it. How long has it been since you last went to the city?"

"Since 2009."

"So you've decided to break out of your isolation?"

"Yes. I'll be going from micro-isolation to macro-isolation! We recluses are alone whether we join the crowd or stay by ourselves."

"What's the use of going out, then?"

He didn't say anything. He gave a barely perceptible smile as he stared at the floor. He seemed to be scrutinising the soft woollen carpet, thinking up some theory inspired by its intricate oriental designs and interwoven colours. Maybe he was thinking about the golden ratio, or the shape of the mandala, or the mysterious symbols of the relationship between decorations and time, place, and the magic of mathematics.

Nuha decided she'd have to rethink her initial impression of him as prudish and rigid. It had been rash of her to conclude such a thing about him based on incomplete information. People are always inclined to rush to judgment based on initial observations, and they usually try to defend this tendency of theirs.

Nadir looked up and, with a hint of hesitation, said softly, "I may go out the day after tomorrow."

"Why don't you wait for me, and we'll go out together?" Nuha suggested. "By that time you will have heard from your friend about that craftsman, and Aunt Hana can give us a ride."

"But if we go out, it's going to be a long jaunt on foot. I'm a walker.

I used to walk for hours at a time. I'd wander up one street and down another, meditating on the world, surrendering to my thoughts and recalling things I'd read. As you know, there's a connection between walking and sound thinking. Walking renews a person's physical and creative energy. So, since I've been deprived of walking down busy streets for so long, do you think you can put up with a long hike? I want to breathe in all the smells and see all the sights, both the pretty ones and the ugly ones. I've had poor eyesight for quite some time, and anyway the sights that have been available to me have been limited, to say the least. Since the time I decided to withdraw from the world, all I've seen have been the walls of my house and garden. I envy you having seen the world and come back again. In any case, you're going to come walking with me."

"I'll be on time."

"You can hold me up if I go into shock over what's happened to the city or the sights I see. Or at least you can keep me from having a panic attack after all these years of being alone."

Nuha saw something uncanny about everything that had been happening, and it seemed to be pulling her toward a place and a time other than her own. It tickled her pride that Nadir had placed his trust in her, and she wanted to be worthy of it. She guessed he must be about ten years her senior, though there were moments when he seemed older than that. She looked at him as he spoke, and felt a tenderness well up inside her at the sight of the subtle lines around his eyes and mouth. She thought: *He's like a stubborn little boy. Or like a man who's punishing life, and being punished by it in a never-ending vicious cycle. He's like a prisoner who revels in his confinement. Or was she jumping to conclusions? Had she misjudged him again?*

Front cover of the novel

Rapping loudly on the door, Hana shouted: "Manal! Nuha!

Open up!"

Manal rushed to open the door, and Hana burst in with her usual clatter.

"Good afternoon, Nadir. Hurry, bring the coffee quick, Manal. I'm so sick of this tooth pain! It seems I've started to get old before everybody else, and it's not fair! The doctor told me he was going to take my tooth out. Have I gone old and decrepit that fast? A little justice for deprived folks like me, Lord!"

"That's enough complaining," Manal told her. "You're still a pretty young thing! Now calm down, or your toothache will come back. I'll serve the coffee with a dessert I make out of walnuts, honey and apples. It's out of this world. You'll love it."

"I can't have anything for two more hours."

Manal left the room and came back carrying a coffee tray that held a plate of apple walnut tarts. She set the tray down in front of Nuha and Nadir and presented Hana with a small cardboard container.

"This is for you to have at home," she explained.

"I envy you this generous, tender-hearted sister, Nadir," remarked Hana.

"And I envy you your jolly temperament," he returned. "Wherever you go, you spread exuberance and laughter. You've been that way ever since I met you, when you first became friends with Manal."

"Thank God I've got something for people to envy me for!" rejoined Hana light-heartedly. "So, have you figured out a solution to the phonograph conundrum that's been keeping everybody so busy? It's practically become an international crisis at my sister's house!"

"And did you think that would be too hard for Nadir?" he teased.

"Well, then, I was right to tell Nuha about you!"

"She and I are going out the day after tomorrow to solve it."

Note:

1 The opening quote from Picasso is taken from a lecture he gave on Cubism with American critic Marius de Zayas in 1923. It was later translated with permission and published in *The Arts* as "Picasso Speaks".

Excerpted from Lutfiya al-Dulaimi's novel
Ushshaq wa Fonograf wa Azminah,
published by Dar Al Mada, Baghdad, 2016

ALI ABDULAMEER EJAM

Lutfiya al-Dulaimi: Sumerian noblewoman on a balcony

Feminist writing in Arab culture has generally been afforded a privileged position of sorts. This is not necessarily due to a particularly high quality of literary production, but rather to considerations external to the profound dimensions of literary writing, in its capacity as a stance on life and the world and as a disciplined craft marked by a solemnity bordering on severity. There has always been a 'social' context that fosters a predisposition to praise a female poet in particular, or a female writer of prose in general, without looking carefully at the genuineness and aesthetic power of her work's literary impact.

Nevertheless, there is an example in contemporary Iraqi (and the broader Arab) culture of a female literary figure whose writing not only demonstrates a high degree of professionalism and commitment, but, in addition, articulates a serious stance on life and the world. The example to whom I refer is novelist and translator Lutfiya al-Dulaimi.

Her first literary work, *A Passageway to Men's Sorrows* (*Mamarr ila Ahzan al-Rijal*) – a short-story collection published in Baghdad in 1970 – is separated from her most recent, the novel *Lovers, A Phonograph and Times* (*'Ushshaq wa Fonoghraf wa Azminah*, Dar Al-Mada, 2016), by nearly half a century of tireless effort. This effort, which has taken the form of books, articles, monographs, and even dramatic works, serves as an indication of the richness and depth of her intellectual worlds, which embrace a concern for issues as varied as womanhood, national identity, and the pursuit of history (Mesopotamian history in particular) via a panoply of unique destinies. Her two latest historical studies, *My Cities and My Passions* (*Muduni wa Ahwa'i*) and *Cities' Diaries* (*Yawmiyat al-Mudun*), embody transformations that are both personal and national in nature. For not only do they familiarise us, both geographically and on a more human level, with cities she has visited as a tourist; they also introduce us to metropolises to which she has travelled out of necessity and which, as such, have become places of exile.

In her novelistic production, which includes works such as *The World of Lonely Women* (*'Alam al-Nisa' al-Wahidat*, 1986) and *Saturn's Ladies* (*Sayyidat Zuhal*, 2010), we are confronted with the struggles of Iraqi women whose contemporary calamities mingle with those of their Sumerian sisters of yore, their destinies rising out of the ashes of tragedy as signs of a life that can never be extinguished, despite all that has afflicted them over the past few decades. As al-Dulaimi explained in a recent interview:

"These women's efforts have suffered serious, and even deadly, setbacks, as many of the relative successes they achieved during the '50s, '60s and '70s have been effectively thwarted. It is easy to see how the religious tide supported by the fundamentalist mentality embedded in political and religious discourse has destroyed the space that a certain timid liberalism had carved out for these women during those decades."

After her home in Baghdad, which had long been a haven for cultural and aesthetic expression, was raided by US forces, al-Dulaimi left for Amman, Jordan, where she has lived for a number of years.

Hope, not Optimism

When producing literary works, al-Dulaimi relinquishes neither her aesthetic nor her social-ethical standards. She comes to the defence of fellow Arab women for whom, as she puts it:

". . . legal strictures have worsened to the point where they are in danger of forfeiting all the gains they had made in defence of their human dignity, social standing, and civil rights. But we have to hold on to some degree of hope, though without false optimism. The phrase 'hope without optimism' comes from British literary theorist, critic and philosopher Terry Eagleton, who used it as the title of one of his most recent books."

Drawing on a spiritual energy that extends back to the women of Sumeria, al-Dulaimi's literary, intellectual and psychological approach to the modern world's most pressing concerns is infused with passion and vison. An additional avenue for her passion and vision is that of translation from English into Arabic, which she has undertaken with perseverance, seriousness and rigour, beginning with her translation of Yasunari Kawabata's *Snow Country* (*Bilad al-Thuluj*, Baghdad, 1985) and concluding with the memoir of Indian president A. P. J. Abdul Kalam, *My Journey: Transforming Dreams into Actions* (*Rihlati: Tahwil al-Ahlam Ila A'mal*, Baghdad, 2017).

The Virtues of Modern Aesthetic Knowledge

Between the earliest and most recent of her translations, al-Dulaimi has provided us with many others of great importance. One such example is her Arabic rendering of *Dreaming to Some Purpose*, the autobiography of author-philosopher Colin Wilson (*Hulmu Ghayatin Ma*, Baghdad, 2015), which I personally consider to be the best thing I've ever read in Arabic about the author of *The Outsider*. This work highlights a number of Lutfiya al-Dulaimi's intellectual virtues, two of which I shall presently examine.

Wilson's autobiography introduces us to a young man who doesn't hesitate to work the lowliest, most grueling jobs for just a few pounds a month. In addition to his unparallelled perseverance, determination, patience and endurance, he is dedicated to a search for knowledge that turns him into an insatiable reader and music aficionado, whose quest for understanding sparks an inquiry into the human enterprise, past and present. In this translation, al-Dulaimi presents the various generations of our country's intelligentsia – most particularly its youth, who seem to balk at discipline, seriousness and hard work, whether in their practical lives or in the pursuit of knowledge – with an inspiring example of diligence, resolve and grit.

Heavy in content and profound ideas, *The Physics of the Novel and the Music of Philosophy* (*Fiziya' al-Riwayah wa Musiqa al-Falsafah*, Baghdad: Dar al-Mada, 2016) is a collection of interviews, translated into Arabic, with an elite group of novelists and thinkers, female and male,[1] who have established an intercontinental presence for themselves, and who are distinguished at once by their ethical, intellectual and aesthetic refinement. Contrary to what it may suggest, the phrase "the physics of the novel" does not mean that this is a book about the technical aspects of novelistic writing. Nor does the term "philosophy" mean that it deals with these writers' intellectual leanings or the 'philosophy' of their literary output. Rather, more broadly, it restores prose to its rightful, intimate, and essential role; namely, that of mirroring the social impact of culture and of writing in particular.

This work marks an anthological introduction to the world's great writers and writings. Professor al-Dulaimi's introductions to the interviews are rich with insightful critique and literary and anecdotal information. As such, it is reminiscent of the old Arabic pocketbook, or the "mini-encyclopaedia" familiar to Iraqis.

In her polished, conscientious translations of the two works discussed here, Lutfiya al-Dulaimi conveys the image of a highly competent, gifted, serious, magnanimous author who is a complement to her gender, and who cultivates a profound openness to the contemporary world and a willingness to engage meaningfully with it. Similarly, throughout her literary career as a writer of stories, novels and academic research, Lutfiya al-Dulaimi has demonstrated the ability to traverse boundaries of time, and to persevere in a gruelling journey driven by the quest to understand human beings in their ascent and their demise, in progress and retreat.

She is a Sumerian noblewoman on a balcony, surveying the contemporary world.

Translated by Nancy Roberts

Note:

1 Those interviewed include: Iris Murdoch, John Maxwell Coetzee, Rebecca Goldstein, Anita Desai, Khaled Hosseini, Ngugi wa Thiong'o, Orhan Pamuk, Chinua Achebe, Toni Morrison, Joyce Carol Oates, Margaret Atwood, Eduardo Galeano and Carlos Fuentes.

AHMAD ALI EL-ZEIN

The Seer

EXCERPTS FROM THE NOVEL *AL-ARRAFA*

TRANSLATED BY JONATHAN WRIGHT

When I was young, I was with my mother in the perfume market and I stumbled at the sight of Yasmine, the neighbours' daughter, turning down the lane and disappearing. My mother said: "Be careful, boy, love is blind." Now I say to her: "Love may be the only thing that has helped me see clearly, mother. We can't see unless we've been love-struck, or have fallen in love."

What a beautiful thing to do: I fell in love. The only form of falling where you don't end up at the bottom of a hole.

Before this first fall of mine, as she dragged me to school one autumn morning like a beast being dragged against its will to some unknown fate, she asked me what I wanted to be when I grew up.

"I don't want to grow up," I replied, firmly and without hesitation.

She repeated her question at the end of the year: "What do you want to be when you grow up?"

"I want to be a writer," I replied with a certain conviction.

As she combed my hair with her slender fingers, she said: "You can write a book only when you've lost something."

I don't remember her later asking me anything about my dreams and aspirations. As if she could see the outlines of the path I would take, she left me to the vicissitudes of fate. Mothers are seers guided by their hearts.

The Tree of Friendship

My name is Suhail al-Attar and I'm from the city of Tripoli. I can trace my ancestry to a family of apothecaries and perfumers, the last of whom was Shihab al-Attar, my great-grandfather and my father's

Ahmad Ali El-Zein, Abu Dhabi Book Fair 2017, photo by Samuel Shimon

namesake. This ancestor of mine was a man of pleasure as well as a trader in perfumes and cloth. He knew how to extract aromatic essences for the women of the city. He mixed lemon blossom water and jasmine water and violets and added pieces of sandalwood that he brought with him from India in bottles with stoppers of pine resin. He matured them in the cellar for a year, like wine.

One of the things that my father inherited from my grandfather, who shared my given name Suhail, was a small box of these perfumes, in turquoise-coloured, pear-shaped vials. The vials sat in velvet bags and came with a little papyrus leaflet describing in Kufic script the spiritual and physical benefits of the perfume, along with pictures by al-Wasiti, inspired by *A Thousand and One Nights*. When my turn came I inherited this box, which contains a hundred little bottles of perfume. I haven't been extravagant in my use of them. They serve only as presents to women whose bodies respond to the exciting wintery fragrance.

I have been in love for long periods, so there is plenty of it left.

So from my grandfather I inherited the perfumes and from my father, a bookseller, I acquired the habit of leafing through books, which have in themselves caused me much exquisite torment, to use a phrase coined by my close friend Adil al-Shawwal, a historian of Andalusia and Palestine. I don't envy Adil his association with these two lost causes, but I love him like a twin – despite our slight disagreements on intellectual questions of no long-term significance.

My name Suhail, which refers to the star Canopus, makes me distant and lonely. I have experienced two periods of abject loneliness: the first after my wife Salma was killed by a sniper's bullet on the Museum road in Beirut during the civil war, and the second after the disappearance of my seer, Nahla Shahoub. I loved them both like crazy and they disappeared from my life in a flash. Between the two deaths many years and many sad events came and went, like clouds blown by wild winds. I grew used to such events, just as trees grow used to having some of their branches torn off by the wind and remain standing with the ones that are left. I haven't had any other option. I have taken to writing to dispel some of these sorrows. I know that writing is no cure, but sometimes it relieves the pain, or at least gives the impression that it does.

In my childhood I learnt from my mother how to draw letters and birds on the dresses that she sewed for the local women in the old market and for other women who came from Tripoli port and were more ready to accept fashions that showed a little flesh – a glimpse of cleavage or the curve of a leg.

Georgette was the boldest in this respect and wore revealing clothes that drew attention to her physical assets. Georgette was blonde, voluptuous and proud of having a Greek sailor called Ritsos as her lover. This Ritsos had nothing in common with the Greek poet, except the name and the fact that he liked flowers. I discovered this aspect of the poet when I was working on *al-Shaab* newspaper and was assigned to interview him. I was accompanied by his translator, who advised me to bring him a bunch of flowers.

The other Ritsos had a bar not far from the harbour in Tripoli, where a coterie of leftists and intellectuals met. I went to the bar when I was grown up and my mother allowed me to discover the city, provided I kept company with intelligent people. This criterion always puzzled me. How could I tell intelligent people from those who were less discerning? Anyway, I don't know how I ended up in Georgette's bar. Maybe she took me there once to listen to Ritsos talk about his adventures in the North Sea off the Dutch coast. His description of Amsterdam, crisscrossed by canals and with its elegant women, made me want to sail off to this unknown world. With my repeated visits to the bar I grew accustomed to the place and often listened to debates on class struggle and historical materialism. I didn't pay much attention to class struggle issues: I was more attracted to the idea that mathematics is not only the science of number and quantity, but also a formal language that aspires to universality. These mysterious concepts stimulated my imagination like magic. This theory later helped me to study more thoroughly the dance of the dervish who performed in the old market. I would follow him as he wove his way through the lanes, twisting his body as he went. If you broke his dance down you would find that it consisted of overlapping circles, and that the points where the circles briefly came into contact formed a force-field that produced ecstasy in the soul. I wrote down this philosophical analysis later, in the course of my meditations on existence, after I had trained myself to think and to establish a relationship between dervish dances and the rotation of heavenly bodies.

What a surprising game it was.

Georgette the bar-owner had started to fold up the last years of her fifties, like the stylish dresses arranged in her wardrobe. Her only role in these sessions in the bar was to provide drink and shyly join in when they asked me to sing some of my grandmother's love songs or pieces I had remembered from listening to my mother's radio – songs by Salih Abdel Hay, Sheikh Zakaria Ahmed and Umm Kulthoum.

I remember clearly that I drew many letter *nuns* on the dresses my mother made. That was before I started to take an interest in phonetics and understood some of the secrets of language. In my childhood I had trouble putting the *hamza* on top of the letter *alif*. It was hard to pronounce in the first place, though not to draw. It seemed to stick in my throat, but I thought it extremely beautiful, reminiscent of a hungry sparrow, with something sentimental and mysterious about it.

I'm fascinated by the way sounds are reduced to these symbolical equivalents.

In later years I often tested my throat by articulating the sounds that make up the extraordinary language in which we register all the thoughts that occur to us – everything that is evoked by the incidents in our lives, by the misdoings of mankind or by our powerful imaginations, which spark like winter coals in the brazier in my grandfather's mansion, high on the shoulder of the valley overlooking Tripoli.

Time has taught me to stay close to the margins, not to avoid them, so that I don't lose my humanity in the body of the text. And Salma my wife taught me to understand music and how to listen to harmonies. She was a piano player and a soprano in the university choir. On the wall she hung a sign saying: 'When the music stops the city walls will crack.'

When she was killed the walls of my soul cracked.

As for my seer, Nahla Shahoub or Ninsumun (she uses both names), she reads palms under her second name and uses her first name when she does sociological research, which is a strange paradox. She taught me the most bitter of lessons: cunning, the eternal nature of the mirage, which lures and draws thirsty creatures to non-existent water. I asked her who named her Ninsumun, and she said: "I chose the name for myself, after the mother of Gilgamesh, the seer queen who sent the temple-prostitute to the forest to tame Enkidu, but then Enkidu became friends with her son Gilgamesh. Enkidu died after a while and in fact he was killed gratuitously for the sake of the Other, and then Gilgamesh went looking for the flower of immortality in the land of Dilmun. Ninsumun managed to tame a friend for her son but she succeeded in making him immortal only in the legend."

There are mothers who lay out the paths their sons should take. And there are women who lay ambushes for their lovers on the bends in those paths.

When a man loves his seer, he submits completely and willingly and is lured into a trap. My mother warned me against this but someone like me has no other option.

I met Nahla Sahoub at the American University of Beirut at the beginning of my academic life, after giving a lecture on migration and the burdens of memory. I spoke about the things that people carry with them in exile or on journeys, things that can be passed on from one generation to another, things that don't complicate the planning or the travelling, light things that don't take up space or require physical strength, stripped down like sounds which are easy to carry, which don't break one's back and can be stored in one's mind. I thought back to the love songs that my grandmother carried in her mind, like the tattoo she had on the back of her hand.

The wind blew from the north
O girl from Maarrat al-Nu'man
Embrace this life with your hands
As if it were cold

This grandmother of mine, apart from having Bedouin origins, also had some Italian forebears. I'll tell that story later. It's extraordinary that I have a genealogical connection to the place where once, at the end of the 20th century, I met a Florentine walking across the Ponte Vecchio and shouting at people: "Make way! I'm walking!" He was walking on giant crutches. I shall also tell the story of this walker.

At sunset in that distant autumn, the disc of the sun was divided by a thin line of inky cloud. Nahla said: "Your grandmother's love song wrenched my heart, bowed my back and took me back to my first home, to the desert where I once lived." Nahla leaned her head towards me and began to steal my heart.

She, the seer, shares with the Bedouin women only their accent. She has started to use it sometimes because she knows that it saddens me, twists and wrings my heart.

Nahla isn't a seer like the ones who roam the streets in search of a party where they can swindle people. Most of those had dark brown faces and tattoos on their chins and their wrists. They would have a gold tooth and carry coloured prayer beads. They wore cheap fake jewellery and called out: "Fortune-teller! Come and have your fortune told!"

This phenomenon was common during the successive wars in my country. Whenever the state collapses, astrology, magic and hocus-pocus spread. Men grow long beards and fortune-tellers of various kinds proliferate. People resort to superstition and the supernatural. Like people drowning, they cling to ropes of air, and the fortune tellers are fully prepared to take on this task. They throw ropes to those seeking hope, to those trying to win back a lost love or a livelihood that has been destroyed.

She wasn't at all one of that kind. I didn't call her my seer to commemorate the women who were seers to kings and emperors, who decided the course of the empire's wars and read fortunes for invaders and army commanders and for the women they loved who waited on the border for the victors to return. The seers were prophetesses in the civilizations of the old world and Sajah was one of them: she set a love trap for Rahman al-Yamama, the self-proclaimed prophet Musaylimah, in order to gain the status of prophetess. In the end they both lost their lives and recognition as prophets, but gained love.

I didn't call her my seer for any of these reasons. I did so to win her love and for fun. I loved these linguistic adventures. Yes, we had fun, and that is one aspect of my character – to attach labels and names to other people and play with the world. I love to challenge the world in this way.

Many people thought she was from the Scandinavian steppes when we were hanging out on Bliss Street, or that she was a lecturer in linguistics. Some people called her Marilyn when she smiled flirtatiously or did her hair in the style of a film star. She too liked to play this impersonation game.

When I sang to her the songs my grandmother used to sing, her origins emerged like a film developed in a laboratory, and signs of the old paths she had taken showed on her face. The singing touched her and she was delighted, saying: "My God, my God." This appeal to the deity was her catchphrase. She said it twice, fleetingly, and her eye flashed with the wonder of a child who has just seen snow for the first time. Then a tear of nostalgia or longing rolled down her cheek – nostalgia for herself as a girl, sleeping there in her grandmother's room and listening to the desert night. In the other eye another tear glistened that seemed to me to be postponed for another departure that would come later.

That sunset I thought back to my grandmother's love songs, which helped my meeting with Nahla turn out as I had hoped, and I sang:

The wind blew from the north
O girl from Maarrat al-Nu'man
Embrace this life in your arms
As if it were cold
There are people who told a story
In a book called time
About a girl coming on a horse
Bowed like sadness
And high as a standard
With one hand holding Hama
And one holding Damascus
And in her heart a boy, murdered
On the edge of the Houran plain

My grandmother's song referred to the 1920s, when her brother had been killed in Houran at the time of the Arab revolt. "At that time," she said, "I was in Damascus with my relatives, whose house was close to the Azm Palace in the Sidi Amoud district. The area was burned down, including the palace, and not a house was left standing. We fled and walked out into the big wide world. The area became known as The Fire and we walked right through the smoke."

The palace was repaired, but not my grandmother's sadness.

"The day my grandmother sang this poem," I told Nahla, "the poplar trees swayed and the birds fell silent because the sky turned overcast in the afternoon and there was a downpour."

They said at the time that the world wept. My grandmother's voice had made it sad.

"Come on, come on," said Nahla, leaning her head towards me and stealing my heart again. "Give me your hand."

I put out my hand and she held it, examined it and said I would have a long life and that my heart was ready for love. I was frightened at first and delighted on second thoughts. When our affection took root, I offered her a vial of the perfume I had inherited. It was turquoise in colour and shaped like a pear. She said: "It's shaped like a female body." I said: "I want to taste it, to taste the pear."

It wasn't a bad beginning to that sunset, just before a stormy night. She read my palm for me. She opened my palm like a page in a holy book that no believer had leafed through for ages, left to chance, neglected. Her hand felt silky and limp like the first autumnal morning, and her fingertips were moist, reminiscent of a line of poetry by Abu Sakhr al-Hudhayli:

> *As if my hand were moist if I touched it /*
> *And fresh leaves would sprout at the fingertips*

I turned my hand over and she squeezed it to make the lines show up. She read the life line and the fate line.

"You're watery and sentimental like the whales in the ocean."

"Will I kill myself like the whales?" I asked. "Come out of the water and beach myself and die?"

"No, you won't do that because you love the world, and you're lucky," she said. "Lucky of course because I met you. You'll survive," she added with a laugh.

She knew what she wanted. She looked away, as if something had unexpectedly fallen and had caused a flash of light. This made her stare into the distance, where the blue of the sea receded gradually, streaked by the rays of the orange sun disk, between the branches of the university's ancient trees, where women students spread out in the shade and novice lovers confided their heart's anguish to them in whispers.

What happened was that the disk of the sun sank into the sea off Beirut.

When she'd finished reading my palm, she kissed it and kissed the fingertips, and I could smell the ancestral perfume. She seemed to come from the same stock as a coterie of people obsessed by the desire to change the world: "An echo of the cry for justice". Adil delighted in this term.

Nahla was like a ray of light when I opened the front door for her. Her body was full and pear-shaped, bursting with passion. Her smile fluctuated between contentment and anticipation. Her eyes was sleepy as though she were looking at a mirage and could see the tail end of a caravan whose departure was mysterious and painful. In the morning she looked more innocent. When we wake up in the morning we all seem to be reborn with a certain innocence, before we fall into the snares of the day and the temptations and dirty tricks of wily cities, the hell of other people, the traps of nostalgia, memory and so on.

I fell into the trap.

And what happened happened.

I think it was an easy beginning for those who wanted to make my acquaintance.

Statement of Profession

By vocation I was a professor of philosophy who believed in the virtues of logic, like Bolzano, the Catholic cleric, but I am no longer like that. Kant fascinated me initially, until I found what I sought in scepticism, even about things that are visible and evident. I no longer read things as they appear. The first strands of my relationship with Marx were woven in Georgette's bar in Tripoli port, where cigarette smoke mingled with the smoke of ideas and with the enthusiasm of Abu Rida, whose passion for the impossible task of changing the world peaked with his third glass and waned with his fourth. He would always begin: "September comes and goes between us and the colour lilac dies on the plain." Okay, he loved a woman in the villages of the highlands whom he named the snow woman.

There in that bar I was struck by an obsession. With a pencil I started to draw a road through the woods and I drew the faces of some companions with whom I would go through them. Whenever I walked a mile, some of their faces would fade and disappear. In the end, years later, when I looked back to see who was still with me I found myself rambling alone down Bliss Street in Beirut, following a trail of scent from the remnants of my seer's perfume, the ancestral perfume, and the phantasms of my companions of the end of the 20th century.

Of all the companions with whom I wove a hypothetical friendship, the most prominent was Russell. I discovered him in my father's library, sitting next to Descartes, Hegel, Marx and others from various historical periods – Heidegger, Descartes, Rimbaud the poet, Taha Hussein, with a sculpture of Abou al-Alaa and a statue of Abu Nuwas in the middle of them, holding an empty glass on the bottom of which was written:

When would you be content with the world in any way
If you are not content with it when euphoric?
Have you not seen the pure essence of the world
And how it emerges from the blazing water?

There were many of them, dozens of them, and they looked like they were in a souvenir photo; all of them had spilled out of their books like water and given a drink to the pilgrims among those passing by on this planet.

They are the water bearers of the paths across the wasteland.

I was pleased with Russell's definition of himself as a satirist rather than a philosopher, because I find rigorous philosophy to be like a desert plant. What strengthened my relationship with this satirist, Russell, is that he was jailed at the end of his life as a supporter of communism, and I was imprisoned early in my life as a sceptic. I go back to this gang whenever I miss my father, and so most of them have stayed close to my pillow, yawning out of boredom with a useless world.

My father used to say: "All those people are descendants of Ibn Rushd." I have no objection if my father wants to trace their theoretical ancestry in this way.

Unfortunately I engaged in this noble mission – teaching philosophy – in the second half of the 20th century, a century of major crimes and tragedies, committed with equanimity and resolve, as a result of an intellectual perversion that is difficult to understand and that was possibly the most terrifying in history. The whole world veered completely off course like a carriage that derails and rolls into a steep valley to be smashed to pieces. The sound of people screaming and mothers wailing will ring through the universe forever. The desert winds keep exposing and then burying the skulls and helmets of soldiers who lost their way. The winds sweep up the sand and the paths of their wanderings are flanked with hastily dug graves arranged any old how and decorated with strips of cloth frayed by the thorns and the wind. I have been to these places in the company of Frederick Olivia the archaeologist and the historian Adil al-Shawwal. We were on a research trip, spending the nights in a bus equipped for this exploratory trip, and during the day we pursued the quest for those who were lost and buried in the sands. We were on assignment for the United Nations, preparing a book on the victims of war in the Arabian deserts.

I woke up one night in the desert to a sound like that of a flute, throaty and monotonous. Then it was joined by another high-pitched sound, and another that was more mellow and less sharp, then it was backed by a fourth and a fifth, and the sound multiplied successively and rapidly, as if some creatures were calling each other to assemble. It sounded then to us as if thousands of musicians were blowing into their instruments and flocking in from distant places. The night was coming to an end and it was hard to make out the source of these sounds. I felt a numbness spread through my body, caused by fear. Frederick said it was the end – the end of the world. I looked at Dr Shawwal. He was mumbling and sweating, his head bowed. I assumed he was reciting the two spell-like incantations, the ones known as *The Lord of Creation* and *The Lord of the People*. Frederick seemed paralyzed when he said it was the end of the world. The sounds grew louder and then faded, came closer and then moved away. They came from wind instruments, some of a fragile nature and others robust. I was certain of that, but I hadn't expected or imagined what I saw when dawn broke.

It revealed a cemetery of helmets and skulls in front of us, stretching as far the eye could see for thousands of yards. The wind was blowing through them and producing this unworldly whistling. What I saw was like the work of a novelist with a powerful imagination, with a talent for putting things in unnatural positions and arrangements that were at odds with the real world, or that of an artist such as Dali. But this has made me depressed all my life since.

After pulling himself together, Adil said: "It looks like the obsession with religion and power turned even wilder when science triumphed, Suhail. The paths to power converged smoothly with the paths to the unknown, and reviving dead languages was not motivated by linguistics, as you sometimes like to pedantically claim. In fact, the most violent religious state ever was created in the second half of this century of crimes, and resulted in the biggest displacement of people in the history of humanity, followed by successive displacements of peoples ruled by bloody and dictatorial monsters." Then he pointed at the cemetery of helmets and skulls, which stretched out towards infinity like Wadi al-Salam Cemetery in Najaf.

This was Adil, the historian of the two reversals, gravitating towards rhetoric whenever he found an occasion to make a statement. Adil theorised as I took pictures. Adil thought, while I took pictures and the wind blew through the helmets and the skulls.

I said to myself: "Photography flourished from the start of the 20th century in order to document crime, more than one could have been led to imagine."

When I acquired a camera I got carried away taking pictures of trees, especially in winter when they were bare and lonely. Things that are whole don't deserve to be immortalised in pictures. Their wholeness immortalises them. That's what I thought when I watched the bare branches shaking in winter. And that's how you'll see me taking pictures now. I take pictures of what's left of a mark that indicates a life that has ended.

I'm not happy that I'm associated with this world, or that the species to which I belong has developed everything that makes it more barbaric than it was in its first forest, when man sharpened flints, kindled fires and shouted in alarm at his astounding discovery, paving the way for a series of yet more astounding discoveries, most of which made man even more deadly.

In any case, the gist of my ideas can be summarised by repeating what I used to tell my students: "The absence of philosophy means society will face a long clinical death, or in the best possible case society will be incapacitated, half-paralysed. Its absence is like the absence of music. If either of them fades away, the core stagnates and harmful algae form on it."

At the time I didn't know that time would reveal tangible proof of this opinion of mine. I became the means of clarification. I became the disabled person who observes his own disability and the disability of the world, which is paralysed just as I am.

My other hobby, apart from photography, is playing the oud and singing, though the music of Bach and Mozart still surprises me with its originality. Salma's fingertips on the piano reminded me of the secret genius of hands, but my genes respond to the melodic mode known as the bayati, rather than to harmonies designed for large orchestras, and this stems from my origins. With my heart I hear my grandmother's singing, and with my mind I hear Wagner, Beethoven, Rachmaninov and Bach.

When Salma was killed I felt the piano was like a coffin. I didn't go near it after she was murdered by that sniper's bullet near the museum in Beirut. The instrument lurked in the house under the window that looked out on the American University. Above it hung a picture of Salma at one of her concerts. If I lifted the fallboard out of curiosity, revealing the black and white keys, I felt I was opening the door to a tomb. Immediately I would hear a painful ringing coming from somewhere in the distance, the fifth note in the musical scale, or G. In Arabic it is called *nawa*, and *nawa* means distance, and distance gives rise to longing, and longing gives rise to song, and so the Arabs, during their wanderings behind caravans, sang in the key of G.

Salma used to tell me: "Music helps the Creator manage the affairs of the universe."

When I felt especially nostalgic, I would pick up the oud and start playing enough of the *rast* mode to help my mind tolerate the world, improvising until I had settled my score with my angst. I would sing when passion touched me. I would delight in my own voice and the mists of nostalgia would rise and rise. As for my inclination to meditate, it made me an unsuccessful lover, because I didn't go far enough into the lessons or the seven levels or stages that would take me to a state of catharsis and a sense of oneness with God. I am not Shams Tabrizi or Jalal ad-Din Rumi, and I don't know whether my Attar ancestors had anything to do with Farid al-Din Attar. I haven't risen on the scale to the level of total serenity.

I'm still in limbo.

I want to be here, in limbo, so that I don't lose the world that I love to play with.

Abdo Wazen

Ahmad el-Zein's hero bids Beirut farewell in a wheelchair

In his novel *Al-Arrafa* (The Seer, Dar al-Saqi, 2018), Ahmad Ali El Zein hides behind Suhail al-Attar, the hero of his novel, who takes on the role of narrator. Suhail does this not as Ahmad's double, but in order to write an elegy for the city of Beirut as he knew it and for the events he lived through in the 1980s and 1990s. Here, an elegy refers to an elegy for a place and a time that belong to a collective memory – that is, the memory of the novelist and also of the narrator, who could be either a well-established Beiruti character or a transient. Elegy could also mean a narrative text full of nostalgia for a city that has almost disappeared as certain people have disappeared, or that is entering its spiritual winter along with the protagonist, who has just completed the autumn of his life and is now immobile, living in a room with two real windows looking out over real places and one symbolic, metaphorical window that looks out over his personal past – a past of multiple times and places, including Tripoli, his birthplace.

The room, which might also be a peripheral protagonist in the novel, is in a care home for the elderly, paradoxically called Paradise Hospital. A high chain-link fence separates the hospital from a psychiatric hospital that is visible from the eastern window, while the western window looks out on a music institute with young female musicians, whom he assigns imaginary names. One of them is an Iraqi woman called Rita and he relates to us her tragedy. A life divided between these two worlds turns the narrator into an informer who listens as much as he watches, since he has a musical ear and playing the oud and singing have been his main pastimes. He is also well-read, a professor who has taught philosophy at the American University in Beirut. But he spies on himself, on his past and the people in his past, especially as now he is living in seclusion in his care home refuge, which he repeatedly calls "accursed". It is this act of "spying" that breaks down the walls of his prison and frees him from the bitter reality around him, either when he thinks back to the past or when he uses his eyes and ears to monitor the world outside the windows.

The Old Man's Biography

This old man, who moves around in a wheelchair or on crutches, sets about writing his autobiography. He starts the first chapter with the words: "My name is Suhail al-Attar from the city of Tripoli." In the third chapter he says: "I'll start with where I am – the care home where I have been for about seven years", but he admits that he is writing his autobiography or his memoirs only to "dispel his sorrows". "I know that writing is no cure but sometimes it relieves the pain, or at least gives the impression that it does," he writes. In the course of the text we learn that Suhail al-Attar has written a play and has hidden the manuscript in an envelope, and that his will says it should be published after he dies. He says the play is an audacious socio-philosophical study of religious thinking and of the idea that "keeping people ignorant creates a breeding ground for extremism".

Cover of Al-Arrafa, 2017

At some time during his seclusion in the care home, Suhail discovers that everyone has abandoned him, even his wife Salma, who was killed by a sniper's bullet on the Museum road while carrying her son Ziryab in her arms. Salma bent over Ziryab to protect him and a streak of blood appeared on her white dress. The memory never left him, even after he fell in love with Nahla, the eccentric "seer" who soon disappears mysteriously from his life. His son Ziryab also abandons him, choosing the care home for him and taking him there when his father becomes dependent on him.

The narrator goes back to this slap in the face time and again in view of its tragic nature and because it's the main reason for his isolation in the care home and estrangement from his son. Suhail's relationship with his son contrasts with Suhail's relationship with his own father, i.e. Ziryab's grandfather. In the desolation of the care home the psychologically isolated father never tires of thinking back to his own father, as if to take revenge on his son for the slap in the face, which he cannot forget despite the deep remorse that the son feels. Suhail the father says that when he looked into Ziryab's eyes after the slap in the face he was confused and thought he was looking into the eyes of someone he didn't know and who couldn't possibly be his son and that Ziryab's hand couldn't possibly be the same hand that had played the oud with him. He says: "He slapped me and then started shouting that he wanted to die, along with me and this filthy

American University of Beirut, 2018 — *Photo by Samuel Shimon*

world." But what hurt the father most was the tears that fell from his son's eyes when he bent over him. At that moment the son himself looked like an old man.

Suhail al-Attar the narrator brings back to life his father, a cultured bookseller and voracious reader who spent most of his life in his bookshop in Tripoli's old market, surrounded by the books that he loved, and who had progressive tastes in both classical and modern culture, preferring al-Ma'arri to al-Mutanabbi. By invoking his father, the narrator brings to life Tripoli, the city of his childhood and adolescence – the atmosphere, the perfume market, the area around the castle and the dervish who appeared in Ramadan and danced in his loose gown, and not to forget Georgette's bar, which was a favourite spot for the young leftists who influenced him in his early youth. At the age of almost seventy he also thinks back to his mother, a skilful seamstress in the fashion industry, and Yasmine the neighbour's daughter, whom he watched from the window as she undressed.

The character of Suhail is realistic and wholly credible, as good as flesh and blood, and the same applies to the care home, the psychiatric hospital and the music institute around him. Everything is realistic here, even the people who pass through his memory, or the city as he sees it when he goes out in his wheelchair with Mona his nurse and two friends who also live in the care home: the mad poet Zaman and Peter the footballer, whom Suhail calls "Peter the Second" to distinguish him from his dramatist friend, Peter the First. This extraordinary excursion does in fact seem to be a farewell visit to a city that is brought to life by his final memories, for the novel is above all a novel of Beirut, though interspersed with some memories from Tripoli, the narrator's birthplace.

Al-Arrafa is no more than 240 pages long but it seems to be full of incidents, events, memories, characters and passing faces, making it rather like an album. Yet the narrative game, which might seem fragmented, actually bases its strong unity on just this: fragments of memory, time and place.

Translated by Jonathan Wright

Excerpted from the novel *Al Arrafa* (The Seer),
published by Dar al Saqi, Beirut 2017

AZOUZ BEGAG

Memoirs in the Sun

AN EXCERPT FROM THE NOVEL
MÉMOIRES AU SOLEIL

TRANSLATED FROM THE FRENCH
BY FRANK WYNNE

Photo by Hartwig Klappert, Berlin

My restless night foreshadowed a horrible morning. Barely 7.00 a.m., hands are shaking me awake. I open my eyes. I see my mother's careworn face in full close-up, that look she has when things are bad, dark circles under her eyes.

Something terrible has happened.

Her lips feebly whisper:

"He's gone back to the motorway!"

At dawn, he had crept stealthily out of the house.

My father.

I scramble into my clothes, she urges me on, pushing me with her open hands, as though my father's life or death now depended on me. I feel guilty this morning because of how I behaved the night before.

Last night, while I was working on a presentation about Louis-Ferdinand Céline for school, Papa had been begging me to let him go home to Algeria, criticising me for being an ungrateful brat when he had bought me clothes, a cool red jumper, a pair of football boots, Christmas presents, a bicycle, roller skates, a watch, school books, a guitar and later a recorder for music class at school . . . He rambled on, giving a detailed inventory of every cent he had spent on me, so that I would be sorry for my ingratitude.

He was pissing me off with this litany that cheerily included random items – like the recorder – of which I had no memory. I stood firm. I sensed him gesticulating behind my back for a few minutes. Then he slumped in front of the TV again in his faux Louis XVI armchair, the faithful kingly companion of all his tedious soliloquies for the past thirty years, and fell asleep in mid-sentence.

This is why I feel guilty this morning. I run through the little film scenario he devised to punish me. I picture him getting up and furtively creeping to the front door, silently opening it, the stairs down to the ground floor to avoid the lift, and wandering through the alleyways. He is singing. He is happy. He talks to strangers on the avenue. He passes the Pont des Lumières and comes to the junction of the A7 autoroute by the travellers' shanty town. He clambers over the railing and, with the wail of a newborn baby, throws himself onto the motorway at rush hour; that way, there is no chance he will survive. His honour would be restored in spite of his wayward son.

I feel distraught. But now is no time for remorse, and my mother, ever the pragmatist, gives me another two-handed shove in the back, shouting: "Go on, for God's sake, run! The rain is coming down in ropes!"

No time even to pull on my socks or figure out what ropes have to do with this crisis. Is she afraid he'll use one of the ropes to hang himself from the arches of the Pont des Lumières?

Fuck explanations, I'm obeying orders.

No time to wait for the lift, which, as usual, is being blocked by the spotty neighbour taking his white dog out for a piss. Taking the stairs four at a time, I hurtle down to the ground floor. Once outside I come to a juddering halt. Ravening clouds choke the sky. I've seldom seen a sky so bitter. It scrambles my sense of direction. Which way do I run? I scan the surrounding area, trying to guess which route my father would have taken. I concentrate. I put myself in his shoes, try to think as he would have. I smell trouble. I just can't put myself in the place of the runaway. I am forced to face a shocking truth: I know nothing about this man.

My father.

He is a serial reoffender. He has already made several successful escapes, all of which, until now, have turned out fine, but every time my mother is terrified that this will be his last. A week ago, the police were able to bring him home because he was carrying his resident's card. Ten times she thanks the good Lord, ten times for having come up with this ruse, but actually I was the one who had hidden it in his pocket. In fact, just as I was slipping it in, she reawakened a memory in me.

Some time ago, I went to Algeria with my older brother, Nabil, to a little village near Sétif, "douar Bendiab", where my father was born. I wanted to retrace his life, as they say, to find my roots. It was the first time I had set foot in the bled. I was amazed I hadn't gone before, that for most of my life I had turned my back on my roots. For me, the need to make pilgrimage came late, but I was glad I had made it.

I had managed to convince Nabil to come with me, hoping he too might find himself there.

We wandered into the little village built over Roman ruins by the route nationale that leads into the Aurès mountains. There were scattered groups of flat-roofed houses, a few abandoned farms on which a few sheep still grazed, a garage festooned with the skeletal remains of ancient French cars.

A dry well with a rusted pump.

It was ringed by boundless fields that stretched to the horizon.

I tried to imagine where my father had played with other children, to picture it. I looked for a tree trunk on which he might have carved his initials: B. B. I even asked a few of the old men of seventy or eighty who were sitting outside their shacks whether they had ever known a Bouzid Begag, an emigrant. I was ready to throw my arms around the first man to say, "Yes, of course!" and proudly proclaim, "I'm his son, I am one of you!"

Strangely, they all seem puzzled by this unfamiliar name. "Name means nothing at all to me," a retired town hall clerk said, emphasising the statement with a shake of his head. I was startled by this. What did he mean by "nothing at all"?

Yet this was the sort of inward-looking village whose peace had not been disturbed by outsiders for years, a place where the landscape had never changed until the Aurès mountains that blocked the eastern horizon were eaten away by the quarries that supplied the frantic construction of the country. Hadn't the population increased fivefold since independence?

Disappointed and unsettled, we had been about to turn back, watched from a distance by two dark-skinned, almost black, children in rags, who stood frozen in their doorway, when a man of about sixty came and introduced himself:

"You're in luck. My father, who is a hundred and two and still has all his marbles, has just woken up from his nap. I'll go and fetch him – he's the only one who will be able to tell you, no one else. Come on!"

Hope was reborn. At the age of a hundred and two, this old man was about to reveal to us his precious memories of our father's life.

A few minutes later, the old man, his head wrapped in a thick red-and-mustard turban, floating in his gandoura, appeared, walking by himself, preceded by his carved wooden cane. He slowly sank into his chair facing the Aurès mountains. Whispering into his ear, his son asked whether he had ever known a certain Bouzid Begag in the village, specifying that he was ben Abdallah (the son of Abdallah), who would have left for France around 1950, after the war.

"His two sons have come to ask."

"Why, is he dead?"

I hurriedly told him he wasn't.

Motionless, the old man made it clear that he understood the question. Eyes fixed on the mountains, he racked his memory for a moment before turning back to us. "No," he said. Very clearly. No one of that name had ever lived in douar Bendiab, no Bouzid, no Begag, nor any ben Abdallah, of that he was certain.

"Besides," he even said sardonically, "everyone here is called ben Abdallah."

He meant that they were all of the faithful, that they were 'abd – servants – of Allah.

I didn't like this at all. There was something bitter about the old man's tone.

It was unbelievable. Why would anyone have lied to us about where my father was born? And what reason could he have had for making up a lie that could be exposed at any moment? I refused to accept this answer. I asked the old man the same question, bending close to his ear and raising my voice. To my surprise, he reared up, lifting his cane. I took a step back, fearing he would hit me on the head. He bellowed that if there had been a Bouzid Begag in his douar in 1950, he would have told us. Even in 1939, if we wished!

He did not appreciate my insolence, after all, for my benefit, and to uphold the sacred code of hospitality, he had been willing to explore the 1950s. For a man of one hundred and two, this was tedious exercise, since although for more than a century his memories had been carefully catalogued, each memory was filed in a dusty cabinet marked with a number known only to him.

A strongroom.

The man I was looking for was simply not from around these parts. That was all there was to it. He had nothing more to say. He laid both hands on his cane to signal that we should get out of his sight, his time was short and he wanted to make the most of his last days in this beautiful land where he genuinely had been born and where all those he had know were buried in the nearby cemetery. With a jerk of his chin, he indicated the place of eternal rest.

He adjusted his turban, which had begun to unravel.

* * *

My brother and I were shaken by this irrevocable verdict. We headed home, downhearted. Especially me, because Nabil, as usual, was pretending that he felt no pain, in his head, in his stomach, still less in his past. For someone who lived in the moment, he could not care less about the idea of having no roots. In fact, he said to me: "You're getting stressed about nothing, kid, if you've got no roots, you can't trip over them."

I liked the metaphor, but it did not apply to me, since I believed exactly the opposite. Knowing nothing about my roots was preventing me from growing up. I had been born in Lyons, and the branches of my family tree were French, granted, but I needed to understand my African roots.

So I could grow new leaves.

These roots were not to be found in the village of douar Bendiab that I had dreamt about so often as a child.

As he walked us back to the car, the old man's son took pity on me. I could tell that he would really have liked to help me find myself, the Good Lord awarding him merit points for helping a human being in pain.

His words of comfort were futile. He could not begin to imagine my grief. I was devastated that I had lost the map to my father's identity, but even more so to discover that, in his birthplace, he was a complete stranger. Almost as though he had never been born.

I felt a hole in the pit of my stomach. What about me, was I alive? I wondered as Nabil and I headed back into town, because if my father had not been born where he was supposed to be, then I might just as easily be a ghost, a shadow.

But I was alive. According to the records in our livret de famille, I had a name; a date and even a precise time of birth; a specific place of birth: hôpital Édouard-Herriot, Lyons; height: one metre seventy-five; colour of eyes: brown; no distinguishing marks. I had a father, a mother. I was blessed that, at any time, I could go to the mairie of the third arrondissement, Bureau 12 of civil registry office to apply for a full birth certificate.

In fact, I had requested one in order to apply for my carte d'identité.

* * *

As we left the mysterious douar at the edge of the desert, we passed the Sidi Messaoud cemetery. Shaded by huge, ancient oaks, it was ringed by a wall that was crumbling in places, which was intended to shelter it from the wind and from stray dogs. At the entrance, a broken gate whose upright had buried itself in the earth could no longer be closed. From outside, I could see ancient tombs from the Roman period; these were followed by a great many graves, almost identical, laid out in neat rows, all dating from the black decade of the Algerian civil war; lastly came the others, simple and identical, from the period when the human life cycle resumed, mounds of tawny soil, their epitaphs hand-painted onto stones or wooden plaques.

These graves marked the different strata of the tortured history of Algeria, ancient and modern. I thought we ought to stop and check whether our family name had been carved with all the others but hesitated, fearing I might discover the truth. Choosing to remain ignorant is cowardly, I thought, but it leaves a door open for the imagination.

"What should we do?" Nabil said, "should we go into the cemetery?"

"No, let's get out of here."

I wanted to leave the douar, because had there been no trace of my father's name in the cemetery, I would have had to confront him about his lies when I got back to Lyons.

That was unthinkable.

By the roadside, the two ragged children who had not taken their eyes off us since our arrival watched as we left, snot dribbling from their noses, not a flicker of emotion in their eyes. They were lucky to be from this place, I thought. Just like their father. For a moment, I saw myself in them, it was 1962, I was dressed in rags, standing next to Nabil in a shanty town in Lyons marvelling at the Citroën Traction Avant hurtling past on the boulevard. In those carefree days, we did not question life. We simply lived it. There was a job and a place for everyone in the society of formica and black-and-white television.

Excerpted from Azouz Begag's novel,
Mémoires au soleil, published by Seuil, France, 2018

Georgia de Chamberet

Mémoires au soleil:

"Exile is a language"

The son is preparing a presentation about Louis-Ferdinand Céline, while his father pleads with him to be allowed to return to Algeria. The son ignores his father, feeling both irritated and guilty. The old man sets off on foot at dawn, down the A7 motorway to Marseille from where he can catch a boat home. He is suffering from "Ali Zaïmeur," a disease "that eats up what's left of people's memories, not that there were many to begin with."The son usually finds him in the Café du Soleil, playing dominoes and drinking mint tea with friends.

A researcher in urban sociology at the CNRS and a prolific author, Azouz Begag was born to Algerian parents who arrived in France in 1949. He grew up in an impoverished, mixed neighbourhood in the outskirts of Lyon. His autobiographical novel about his 1960s childhood, *Le Gone du Chaâba* (*Shantytown Kid*, translated by Alec G Hargreaves and Naima Wolf, 2007), was made into a film by Christophe Ruggia. Released in 1998 it received a César Award nomination for Best Debut. As the Delegate Minister for the Promotion of Equal Opportunities in the government of Prime Minister Dominique de Villepin, Azouz Begag publicly fell out with Nicolas Sarkozy after France's suburban riots in 2005.

His poignant biographical memoir, *Mémoires au soleil* (Memoirs in the Sun), is one man's unique and compelling story about the powerful yearning for tradition and family while paying tribute to a remarkable man whom he watches, helpless, decline into dementia. As the son attempts to get to know his father, he investigates the roots of identity, and goes to the heart of the French conundrum.

"We're a family with no history or genealogy, no photo albums or books. We're like extra-terrestrials dumped on earth by an errant spaceship." How to reconstitute a life when memories are hidden?

Azouz and his brother, Nabil, visit their father's birthplace, the village Bendiab which lies in the shadow of the Aurès mountains. It is near the town of Sétif where there was a massacre of anti-colonialist demonstrators in May 1945. They make enquiries at the town hall, but draw a blank. A centenarian who is alleged to be a living oracle affirms that he has never heard of Bouzid Begag, and remarks, "Everyone here is called ben Abdallah." Azouz is upset to discover that he and his brother come from nowhere, although Nabil is philosophical, "The less roots we have, the less likely we'll trip up over them!"

Their parents had met when working on the farm of a coloniser in the village of El Ouricia. The farmer seemed to care more for his horses than his Algerian workers. When the few sheep the young couple possessed were stolen, the decision had been made to emigrate to France. They ended up in Lyon where they had distant cousins.

Bouzid Begag worked all his life in France as a stonemason for a company called l'Avenir (the future) and never took time off for fear of being made redundant. He also wanted to prove to his hosts that he was a decent, honest man. Not only was he illiterate – his official documents were all signed with a cross – but bureaucrats regularly inserted the wrong or misspelled

Poster for the film Le Gone du Chaâba, *from Azouz Begag's novel of the same name.*

name, dating back to the census of 1925-26, and his first carte d'électeur issued in 1948.

At school, a classmate who pinches the son's exercise book to find out his grades sees the father's mark, and is mocking, "Your dad can't write, na, na, na . . . he's called Monsieur X!" Lessons about the Gauls and kings called Louis do not inspire a sense of belonging. Young Azouz wonders what his grandparents looked like. Learning French and acquiring French identity are not one and the same.

His brother, Nabil, is ashamed of his parents, and blots out feelings of unease. He does not believe in God, smokes and drinks, and ends up in prison for a year after committing a violent robbery using a scooter. His aggression and rugby ball-shaped head earn him the nickname "Mental Nabil". Regular incarcerations become a way of life.

In the course of researching his family origins, Azouz Begag discovers three ancestors who fought for France in the Great War, one of whom died in the Battle of the Somme. He also finds the son of the farmer for whom his parents had worked, but their reunion is a disappointment.

Being French of Maghrebi and/or Muslim origin is problematic, regardless of status. French republicanism is based on secularism and universalism and does not allow for a hybrid identity: immigrants are to be assimilated. The hyphenated (or more accurately these days, unhyphenated) identity French Algerian does not exist in the way African American does in the US, or British Asian in the UK. France needs to question its rejection of the "foreign", and to come to terms with "difference".

Mémoires au soleil,
Published by Seuil, Paris, 1 March 2018.
ISBN: 9782021392005. Pbk, 192pp, €17.
E-book/PDF : ISBN 9782021392036, €11.99.

YAHYA WAGDI

Family Photos

A POEM

TRANSLATED BY RAPHAEL COHEN

1

If life was fair
I would have taken Mum to the pub
instead of the cemetery.
I would have introduced you
and smiled when she asked:
"Isn't she the one you were in love with?"
After a couple of drinks, she would admit:
"I told her off once. Ordered her not to call again!"
I would be happy if you both made up.
Maybe I'd sleep afterwards,
sleep like never before!

2

Weddings are like funerals
they're completely the same.
Siblings ranked behind the groom
when tying the knot, and when bearing the coffin.
Relatives . . .
God bless 'em,
aunties inspecting everyone in the throng
overseeing the pregnant women
– and the men who filled their wombs
whispering about the brides' gold.
At both a cleric is essential
and a few prayers!

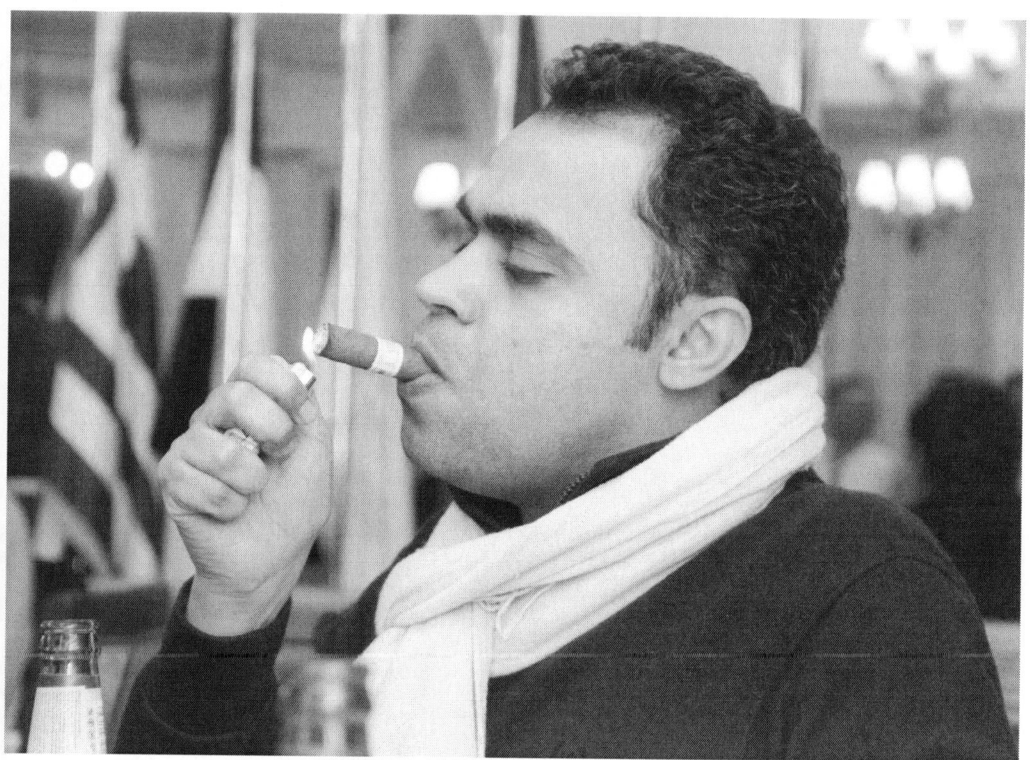

Weddings are like funerals:
at both we cry sometimes
and go home having lost someone!

3

Yesterday night I deleted lots of names from my contacts,
all the dead.
I saw them while trying to call my Dad
and tell him about my new house
in the district he built with his own hands
and never visited after,
except once
when his funeral went through it.

The original Arabic was published in *Ibda'a* magazine,
Cairo, March 2018

ABDELRASHID MAHMOUDI

The Wolf Slayer

A CHAPTER FROM THE NOVEL *AFTER COFFEE*

TRANSLATED BY NASHWA GOWANLOCK

Khalil tossed and turned outside his shop, which overlooked the canal. He batted a fly that hovered over his nose, then dozed off again. The breeze toyed with the hem of his jilbab, as if it wanted to pick up the fabric and fly off. Nothing disrupted the serenity of this scene until a noise surfaced – a cacophony of screaming, laughter, and barking – from the direction of the canal. A group of boys was crossing over while a black dog protested over how they'd charged towards the water without him. The boys were fleeing from the Upper Egyptian locals with their loot: dates, prickly pears, and reeds. Khalil woke up when the boys' commotion reached him, and all traces of sleep disappeared once the afternoon call to prayer sounded from the farthest end of the village. It felt as if a firm hand was shaking him, urging Khalil to get up and go to the mosque to pray on time, but he didn't budge. Those little devils were still running riot, even though they usually panicked and scampered off to their hiding places once the blistering midday hour had passed. After the shame of what had happened with his sister, Khalil felt no desire to do his ablutions or pray. He wished he could sleep and never wake up. He didn't want to talk to anyone about anything. His customers no longer had anything to say to him, either. They each grabbed what they needed before hurrying off. No one would stay and sprawl out on the ground outside his shop any more to play cards, drink tea, and smoke *muassel*. All that had ended, and anyway he didn't want to face them. He saw the question in people's eyes, which nobody dared to utter: 'Where did she go?' Every time a customer appeared, he lowered his head. He had transformed from an intimidating character to a man broken by the weight of shame

Photo by Samuel Shimon

and helplessness, all over what his sister Zakiya had done. What's the use of having a shop and buying and selling when you can't talk to anyone? Wouldn't it be better to stay at home and let no one see your face? He finally stood up to close the shop. But what's the point of staying at home? he wondered. There was only one person to turn to for help: Ibrahim Abu Zaid.

He walked past Nafisa's house. The old woman was outside chasing her chickens with a broomstick – a dried palm branch with its strands still intact – to bring them in for the night. She wouldn't usually do this before sunset, but had decided to bring them in early that day. As Khalil walked by, he turned his head to avoid greeting her. He had started to despise the old woman because his sister used to go to her house and work for free. 'I hope you're well, Khalil,' Nafisa called out to him, but he didn't reply.

'You bear a heavy burden, my boy,' she added, when he was further away. 'God help you, my dear.' Still, the fact that he'd ignored her had stung. She didn't deserve that. Whatever had happened had happened, and she was not to blame. Medhat had also passed by her house a short while ago with his dog and his friends, on their way back from the opposite bank of the canal, brandishing their reed sticks. 'Come here my darling,' she had called out to him. 'Give your Nana a kiss, my love.' But the boy stopped to say with disdain, 'I don't kiss old people.' 'Come here boy, be kind,' she said. 'I'm your Nana, your darling Nana.' 'When you take off your nose ring,' he replied. That scrawny kid is only five years old, she thought as she shook her head. You'd think he was spawned by devils. God rest the souls of your mother and father, Medhat. Then she sighed. 'But then again, who does like old people?'

She was the last of the grandparents' generation. Back when she lived with her late brother's wife, Zainab, she was treated like a queen. But after Zainab died, she went to live with Fatima, Zainab's second cousin, until she grew weary of the way Fatima's daughters treated her. The girls also don't like my nose ring, like Medhat, she thought. 'What is that hanging from your nose, Nana?' they would say. 'No one wears those anymore.' They didn't like the tattoo on her chin, either. And they would never let her utter a single word without making fun of her. 'Nana never stops talking,' they would say, or – even worse – 'My nana's started spouting gibberish.'

They liked her food, sure, they would devour it – all the old recipes she carried in her heart – but they didn't want her to speak. Fatima had asked her to teach her eldest daughter the basics of cooking, in preparation for marriage, but could Saadiya endure her instructions and advice? 'Nana, you're driving me crazy with all this talk about how much water to add to the rice, because you say perfecting the rice is the stamp of a good cook. And the tomato sauce that has to be stewed just so . . . Do you think the man will be as bothered as you? Why can't he just be quiet and eat whatever I cook?'

At first, Fatima would tell her daughters off, but she soon changed. After she got fed up with Nafisa's rambling about her missing son and her relentless, futile appeals to him, she gradually began to let their comments go. Whenever the memory of his absence became too painful, Nafisa would find somewhere private and start crying out, imploring him to come home. After Fatima gave up on her, she gathered her belongings and moved to this house that turned its back to the village, facing the country road instead. Here, no one had any right to complain about her, and she could see out her remaining years in peace. And here, she could wait for her absent loved one.

Thirty years had passed since her son Hashem was whisked off to the provincial jail. It was said the police found him and the rest of the gang because one of them had left behind a sandal as he fled the scene, which is how the police dogs were able to trace them. She had seen one of them return – Musa Abu Mostafa. He had stepped out of the police van supported by two policemen because he couldn't walk on his own. After fifteen years in prison, he was back, but the happiness of his wife and children was short-lived. Shortly after reaching his house, he lay down and never got up again. He died after spending barely a week with his family. When she saw him clambering out of the police van, she knew he didn't have long. Having witnessed pangs of death in both the young and the old, she had come to recognise the meaning behind his pallor.

But her son Hashem never came home, not even after the end of his prison term. The rumour was that he had escaped prison and fled to Palestine. It was also said that he was spotted several times wandering the fields on the other side of the canal, near the Sa'ida, or Upper Egyptian, village. So why hadn't he returned? Hashem, why won't you come back home? She recalled his life from the day he was born, including the time she found him a fiancé, and how she had tried to hasten his wedding so she could become a grandmother, since he was her only son. She would return to her memories of each event as if it had happened yesterday, without skipping a single moment. She remembered the date, the season it fell in, what food she had prepared, and the colour of the chicken's feathers that she had slaughtered for the occasion.

One of Fatima's daughters would interrupt her. 'Nana, do you have to go into so much detail? Do you really have to tell us about the rooster you slaughtered for the guests, how heavy it was, how its feathers were black and that its crest was large?' No one wanted to listen to her tales of sorrow. Ever since she'd started living alone, the days had dragged and the nights even more so. Her visitors slowed to a trickle. Her family began to forget about her. Zaki no longer dropped in on her. He used to stop off after his afternoon nap, before the *asr* prayer, to see if she had anything he could snack on. She would bring him whatever he wanted – a hot loaf of bread, some crushed salt and chilli pepper. Zaki was the only one who was still faithful to the old days, and the only one whose heart still went out to everyone. But she didn't know what had happened to him lately. His visits had dwindled and, when they did happen, they were fleeting. His face seemed permanently strained.

Salama – may God prolong his life and protect him from danger – was the only one in her family who still cared about her. He farmed her land, was content with his share of the harvest – a quarter – and never refused her a single request. He also helped to sell her share and brought everything she needed from the Monday or Wednesday markets. 'The boy is gallant and chivalrous and has a kind heart, but what kind of a nightmare has he caught himself up in?' she wondered. There was no one left but Zakiya – the Baharwa girl – to help her with household chores like kneading the dough, baking, and washing. Guided by the Most Merciful One, she did it all for no wage, even though the Baharwa people were famous for being tight-fisted. Then, the One and Only God ordained that this calamity would fall on her and Salama. Nafisa started to worry that Salama and Zakiya would end up as unlucky as Hashem – he, too, had been kind, chivalrous, and naïve. But still, God had brought a catastrophe down on him, great is His wisdom. She worried they would end up doomed like Zainab's youngest and most handsome child. He was the one known as 'the star' and 'the neighbourhood heart throb', before he was lured by some thugs, became addicted to 'snorting powder', and ended up dying at one of those gatherings. Over the years, she had seen how misfortune only ever remembered the kind ones. Hashem, for example, didn't murder anyone, and none of that gang had any intention of killing a soul. They were a bunch of misguided youths and the devil used them as his playthings. May God avenge them. That gang leader sent respectable kids to hell while he dozed at home so he could escape the consequences as smoothly as a strand of hair teased out of a lump of dough.

They had wanted to rob the home of a widow in the Nazlet Elwan village to steal her silver, but she woke up and confronted one of them, who stabbed her with a knife. It was an accidental blow. But Hashem didn't attack anyone; he didn't clash with anyone and hadn't even gone into the house. He'd been standing guard at the top of the road ready to whistle if he saw anyone approaching. 'Why did you do it, when you came from a good family?' she moaned. 'Did you need any gold or silver? Why then, when you're the one who always gives away everything you have? Why not come home, my son? My heart is tired of waiting, Hashem. They say you come to the other side of the canal at night. So take a little turn, my darling. Say, I'll go and see my mother whose tears have run dry. Hashem, there's nothing but a canal to separate us. You can cross the water by foot . . . They are just a few short steps, my sweetheart.'

When she had managed to usher in the last chicken, she fastened her door shut with a latch and key.

* * *

Hajj Zaki was the first to appear when the worshippers began arriving at the mosque in answer to the afternoon call to prayer.

He circled the building to inspect its condition and reached the back door, pursing his lips with discontent. His brother still lifted water out of the mosque's well to fill the bathing basin, as well as the place for ablution and the latrines. He also raised the prayer call at the regular times with a booming voice that travelled across the canal and was heard at the Sa'ida's village – a beautiful sound that humbled people's hearts. But lately, it had started to cause a tightness in Zaki's chest. And the building was in a deplorable state; the wall by the well had large cracks in it that warned of imminent collapse. He appealed to the Muslims to rescue their mosque before it caved in, but none of the Qassimis or the Baharwa people were interested in his pleas. No one wanted to pull a piaster from their pocket to help repair the house of God. They wanted him to bear the burden on his own, as he had in the past, but he couldn't do it any more. The mosque was old, built in his grandfather's time, and his father had taken charge of its upkeep throughout his whole life. As for the others, their hearts had toughened and their faith weakened. He sighed. The families of the neighbouring villages used to come for Friday prayers, but now their attendance was rare. He recalled painfully how he used to invite everyone after the prayers for lunch at the guesthouse they called the *seera*, serving them lentils in winter and rice pudding in summer. That was in the good old days. An onion shared with a loved one is a lamb, as the saying goes, but this loved one had neither lamb nor onions any more.

He stopped to shoo away the boys who had gathered around the back door. They were carrying sticks made of reed, and some were as naked as the day they were born. The pack started to disperse but two lingered: Medhat and his black dog.

Medhat was rooted to his spot by the door and gazed out at the far corner of the mosque where a rectangular wooden box stood, tipped upright on four legs. They called it 'the coffin'. He would always see it there, in the same place, unless it had been removed by the village men as they hauled someone inside it to a distant place from which there was no return. This had happened when they carried his mother away and when they took his grandmother, covered in a white sheet that fluttered in the breeze. He may never have discovered what all this meant had he not wondered why neither his mother nor grandmother had come back from that faraway place. 'Where's my ma?' he had asked Na'sa, his wet-nurse. 'She went to the market to get you halva and a couple of loaves of special *bandar* bread,' she replied. 'And where's my Nana?' he asked her. 'She went to visit her relatives in Hassiniya,' she said. Oh, how he had waited for his mother to return with the halva and the special bread. And how he had waited for his grandmother to come back from her family visit. But he now knew that Na'sa had lied and that anyone carried off in that box would not be back. That was the distant place they called 'death'.

One of his friends pulled at his arm and another struck him on the shoulder with a stick, but he didn't move. They were gesturing excitedly with their reed sticks because they were on their way to war . . . their mission at this hour was to attack the wasps that built their nests in the straw and firewood stored on the roofs of the houses. They were not deterred from battle by the fact that wasps defended their homes fiercely and were capable of inflicting serious injuries on the attackers – especially the naked ones. The child didn't budge until Hajj Zaki put his hand on his shoulder. 'Isn't it rude to walk around naked like that, Medhat?' 'We left our clothes by the canal,' Medhat replied. 'We sped off when the Sa'ida's dogs started chasing us'. 'All right, but hurry on along now, please,' Zaki said. 'Good-bye.'

The two sheikhs, Hamed and Sayyid, approached, but stepped aside from leading the prayer when they saw Hajj Zaki. It wasn't because he was more educated than them, since he hadn't studied at al-Azhar Islamic University. And it wasn't because he was older, since he was actually younger than them both. It was because they recognised his stature. If he wasn't there, they would have ended up competing over who would lead the prayer and some of the congregation might have sided with one or the other, since they each had their own supporters. The first one, Sheikh Sayyid, had spent God knows how many years boarding at the revered University of al-Azhar without receiving a graduation certificate. As for the second sheikh, Hamed, he had spent only five years at the Religious Institute of Zagazig. Thus Sheikh Sayyid believed, along with his supporters, that it was his right, being the more educated, to lead the prayers. But Sheikh Hamed believed, and so did his supporters, that to pray behind Sheikh Sayyid was an arduous ordeal because he would forever stutter and stammer. And from time to time, he would emit a sound that resembled a cross between a sip and a slurp, and he would end up reciting the rebellious phrase or word over and over again until it obeyed him. Not only that, but these falterings that seemed to haunt Sheikh Sayyid would prompt the boys in the back rows to snigger and nudge each other, or worse. Sheikh Hamed, however, was characterised by his wit and eloquence. Most importantly, he would complete the prayer before the worshippers' patience had completely depleted, knowing that some of them wanted only to carry out the religious obligation in a slapdash manner. And so he would leave no room for the devil to penetrate the rows of worshippers and distract them from their state of submission as they stood in the hands of God.

If Hajj Zaki was present, it meant the end of the dispute; everyone would be in agreement, tranquillity would abound, and the prayer would be performed as it should be. Even Shabana, whose mockery no one could escape,would declare during his gatherings at the village's public *jurn* that 'Saad Pasha and Nahhas Pasha may be the elected leaders of the nation, but my cousin Zaki is the chief of the "sons of Qassim", without election or royal decree.'

But this unelected leadership no longer pleased Zaki, since it had become too heavy a burden to bear. It had somehow been thrust upon him through neither his nor anyone else's will but God's. He was simply performing his duty, just as he had when his father was alive. Back then, he would receive guests generously and would sometimes act on his father's behalf in resolving conflicts. But he just couldn't keep doing it any more; God burdens not a person beyond his scope, after all. He called for the worshippers to straighten the rows as he led the congregational prayer, so that 'God may have mercy on you', and everyone shuffled into position behind him. There was still some respect left. No one complained, no arguments erupted, and the boys didn't nudge each other in the back rows or snigger if the prayer dragged on. And so everyone was humble in the hands of the Sacred King.

The crisis now was that he himself struggled to stay humble and focused. His mind would wander just as he started to recite a verse from the Qur'an, and he would try to remember the next one, but it would only come through arduous effort. Between one verse and another was a gap filled with silence, a gap mired in darkness. Between one verse and another, fear reared its head. And recently – since the quarrel with his brother – these gaps had been growing. If this continued, people would surely abandon him.

Then there was Shabana at the *jurn* gatherings; if people found out about his situation, there was no way he would escape Shabana's ridicule. Fear resided deep inside him, and it surfaced during the prayers, or as soon as he laid his head on the pillow, or whenever he saw his brother. There was a phrase that was desperate to launch itself from the depths of his soul towards his lips in the shape of a scream, but it would always get lodged in his throat. And there were words he wished he could raise to the One from Whom Nothing is Concealed, but he found himself mute.

* * *

The village of the Qassimis, the descendants of the original settler, Qassim, was an odd kind of place, surrounded by secrets on every side. Most of the locals believed jinn inhabited the mosque's well, and it was said that a black, horned serpent guarded the bathing basin of the mosque. Sheikh Sayyid claimed that 'The Enemy' extended his hand and poked him on the right side of his body, trying to nullify his prayers, whenever he performed the voluntary, late-night tahajjud. Beyond the fields that extended south of the mosque was a stagnant pond with algae that rose above the water's surface. People would try to keep their distance as they walked past, because it was said to be deep, bottomless, and inhabited by various types of ghouls. Woe betide anyone who lost their footing and toppled in! The main road that split the village in two ended at the perpendicular country road that bordered the canal. Those were the northern borders of the village. But beyond those borders was the opposite bank of the canal, where the Sa'ida lived. There was some interaction between the Sa'ida people and the villagers, and they would sometimes visit each other. The village children would also cross to the other side on foot when the water was shallow – since the canal was four metres wide at most – or swim across during the periods of flooding. They would climb the Sa'ida's palm trees to steal their fruit in the date season. And they would chop up the reed branches they found floating on the surface of the water to use as spears that they would fling at wasps, or make reed pens to use at the Qur'anic school. Crossing to the opposite bank would fill the boys with fear and, to them, reaching the other side was an adventure to top all adventures.

At the western side of the village there was the waterwheel, shaded by the old sycamore tree whose branches extended over the path. The well at the waterwheel was inhabited and had its own tales of terror. It was said that a man called Abdulhadi had been mesmerised by a female jinn – one of the women of the underworld – while he watered his land one night. She had appeared to him from the well and forced him into an engagement, offering to take him to live down in the abundant bliss amongst her family. But he refused because he was faithful to his wife, the mother of his children. It was also said that he was strong and fought with her until she defeated him. She only managed to overcome him when she embraced him, pressing her breasts into his chest such that two nails protruding from her nipples hammered into him and pierced his heart. When was this? And to which past generation did Abdelhadi belong? And where was his wife whom he had abandoned? And where were his remaining family? These were questions for which no one had answers. It wouldn't even cross anyone's mind in the village – apart from Shabana at the *jurn* gatherings – to ask them. There was another story about a young man called Abdelsalam who was enticed by a female jinn and disappeared with her to live together in her underground world, where they have remained ever since. Who were his mother and father? In which era did he live? These questions had no answer and no one except Shabana thought to raise them, to ridicule the sons of Qassim and to highlight their foolishness.

If ever the water buffalo's hoof slipped when it was in the vicinity of the waterwheel, causing it to topple into the well, it would be taken as an ominous sign and a harbinger of great catastrophe. The women's voices would then ring out as they screamed and wailed, and the men would rush from the outskirts of the village to the helpless animal to try and pull it out. If they failed to rescue it, they would bring a knife and slaughter the buffalo on the spot before it died.

The area around the waterwheel was inhabited, too. There was a spirit that appeared to passersby at night in the shape of a donkey whose back rose higher and higher until it was taller than the top of the sycamore tree and even reached the sky. If anyone approaching from the western side at night was destined to come across a spirit, then they would most likely spot it near the waterwheel and the sycamore tree. And it would be the Satanic donkey that they would see.

This paranormal activity was not restricted to the western side of the country road, since the eastern side had its peculiar stories in turn. There, the spirits would not be limited to nocturnal appearances. Either 'Mother Ghoul' or 'The Summoner' might emerge in broad daylight, and especially during the siesta hour. Everyone would be asleep, and all the animals would appear stunned – the water buffalo, for example, would be powerless to bat the flies pinching at its tail – and the whole area around the *jurn* would be vacant. But people returning from the central market on Wednesday might be unfortunate enough to be heading back during the witching hour and could be half-asleep astride their donkeys when they would suddenly be woken up by the call of 'The Summoner'. Then woe betide those who responded, for the call was irresistible.

The world at large was divided into two: the countryside and the *bandar*. The *bandar* was the world of civilisation and luxury.

The nearest town would not be considered *bandar*, nor would the capital of the province, or the provincial cities in general. Those areas were in between, only partially civilised. Cairo would be classified as *bandar*, and perhaps Alexandria too, since many of its residents were said to be foreigners.

But what was the secret of the spirits' fascination with donkeys? The question was once put to Shabana.

'Donkeys are easy to ride. If someone passing by obeys the devil and rides it, then they're doomed. It's the same with women. A woman entices you until you ride her and end up in hellfire. Ha ha ha!'

He laughed, and so did his audience. But his words seemed to carry a hint of cunning. Was he also alluding to what had happened to Salama and Zakariya?

Published by Hamad Bin Khalifa University Press, Qatar
forthcoming June 2018

Abdelrashid Mahmoudi's novel *Baad al-Qahwa* (*After Coffee*) won the 2014 Sheikh Zayed Book Award in the Literature category.
See, below, page 198, for a review of the book.

Literary Influences

From time to time Banipal invites a prominent Arab author to write about the books and authors that have had an influential impact on their life and work.

Here, the Palestinian author **Liana Badr** talks about how learning to read at a very early age and listening to umpteen stories opened up a "wonderland" that never closed, even after the Six Day War prevented her ever returning home to Jericho, making her a persistent witness and a writer whose core mission was "to see, hear and learn".

LIANA BADR

All I Want to Do is Write

Photo by Ahmad Dari

When I was born, in the city of Jerusalem, my parents chose to give me a name from a contested poem attributed to the 10th century Syrian poet al-Wa'waa' al-Dimashqi. I was my parents' second child – to their great sorrow they had lost the son who came before me. My father was a doctor and my mother a teacher and great beauty who had volunteered to work as a nurse after the bloody wars in Palestine. For my birth they prepared a white gown: on it my father wrote the letters of my name in Arabic calligraphy while my mother embroidered my name in beautiful English letters with silk thread. Maybe they wanted me to see the world from two perspectives: one local, and one more expansive.

And that is what happened. I grew up under the wing of Arabic literature, at the same time as feeling attached to the literatures of the wider world.

Somehow I learnt to read before entering first grade at school. I don't know how it happened, but I often went with my mother, the school principal, to her work and attended various classes with her. I do remember my father discovering by chance that I could read the words in the newspaper headlines. He took this as a cue to start reading me the story of the ant and the grasshopper, whose sad fate upset me each of the many times he read it from the book. He also made sure to show me pictures of dinosaurs and airships.

A new tradition was established in our house: I would refuse to eat lunch unless I could listen to a story in return. If the old women storytellers happened to be at home, I would finish off my food to the rhythm of their tales, but if they weren't there at the time, my mother would impose a punishment that was explicit and invariable: to stay seated, condemned not to leave the table until I finished everything on my plate. What really annoyed me was having to sit in boredom on the chair for two or sometimes three hours. But I put up with this torment patiently even if it lasted that long, until my father came back late from his clinic and began to tell me little stories. At that I would open my mouth and gobble down the food within minutes, indifferent to the fact I was now eating cold, hard lumps that could hardly be swallowed.

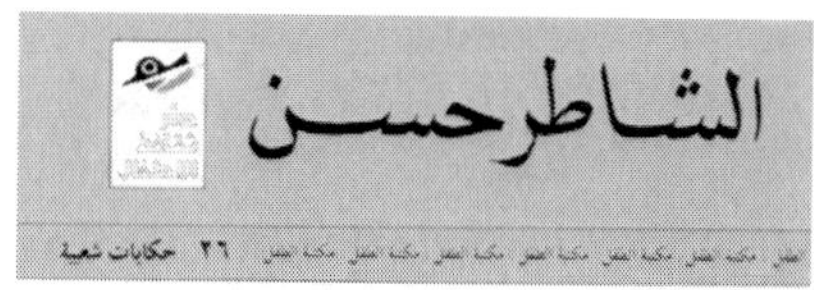

My father's aunts and their elderly women friends, who stayed in our house for long periods in line with the prevailing family customs, stood in as walking human books, recounting stories in abundance, like waterfalls that never stopped. Theirs was a popular culture that was rich in stories, proverbs and mythical creatures such as ghouls and the Amoura – the soul of a murdered person that roamed the streets at night seeking revenge – and all kinds of fantasies that were at once colourful and horrific, like the stories of ghouls devouring human beings. Hebron, a city of stories, a city closed in on itself like a castle on a hill overlooking the south and impregnable to conquerors, had a rich and bountiful popular heritage. I even knew old women from the family who gave young women advice by telling them diverting tales they had just made up, rather than preaching to them and giving them overt moral guidance, which might have alienated the girls from their message.

Al-Shatir Hassan stories

These folktales, then, were my first culture, imbibed from the lovely old women present in my life. My grandmother had died when my father was a child, and it was these women who nourished my imagination with dozens of their stories. As for my father, he made up funny stories for me about al-Shatir Hassan (Clever Hassan), based on the original text but expanding on the theme of a wily hero always rebelling against a hapless sultan.

Later, I began to read any story I came across in the house. Once, fed up that my father and mother were busy with their intellectual guests who never stopped arguing, I came across the novel *Mother*, by Maxim Gorky, and began to read it alone, at the age of five, without understanding any of the content except that there was a mother in it. The words were mysterious. What did 'workers' mean, or 'gathering on the railway station platform', or 'labour and trade unions'? I didn't understand why they were meeting, or why the mother did what she did. The word 'workers' would remain difficult for me for ages, despite explanations by my father, my mother and their friends.

Right after that, in the library at home, I came across a copy of *A Thousand and One Nights*: the Bulaq edition. But that word Bulaq had me stumped. Who was this Bulaq? Was she a woman or what? My mother didn't explain what any of the words meant. In fact, she banned me from reading the book on the grounds that it wasn't suitable for my age.

I liked the books of stories whose vocabulary I could understand and in which I could imagine the places, and I started sneaking onto the kitchen balcony to read them. There then came a succession of books that my mother approved of, such as the series of children's stories by Kamel al-Kilani, known as the Green Library, and magazines such as *Samir* and *Sindbad*. I thought they were like dessert after a meal; because they were amusing and left behind only a hint of the flavours of stories.

A new stage in reading began when I was eleven years old at the Maqdisi boarding school, close to a cultural centre that had a library for adults with plenty of American and international literature. I was granted a special privilege in this library: the right to borrow four books at a time, while ordinary people couldn't borrow more than two. That was because I changed my books so frequently that the nice librarian thought that by letting me take four she would save herself trouble and save me the bother of coming every day or every other day. The fascinating character of Scarlett O'Hara was what gave me my attachment to novels. Through *Gone with the Wind*, which I read in full (one thousand pages in two volumes), I discovered that it is people's stories that make history, and these compelling characters, who are very much like us, who give us insight into events, other

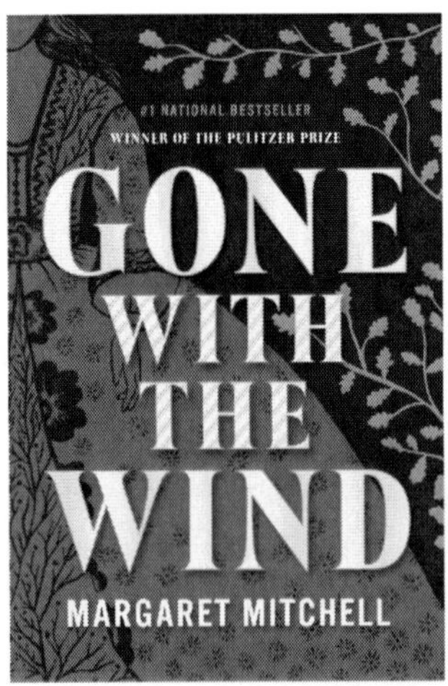

Maxim Gorky

Taha Hussein

Tawfiq al-Hakim

people and ourselves at the same time. For the first time I was reading about wars in other parts of the world. I had thought that war was invented specially for us, to lie in wait under the beds of the Deir Yassin orphans who had been evicted from their homes after brutal massacres. I began to realise it was profoundly important that humans should be free, and should rebel against slavery based on colour, or the slavery imposed by colonizers who seize the land of indigenous populations and have no qualms about killing them, as had happened in Palestine. And so I began to write poetry about what I saw. From there I was drawn to many Arabic and translated novels, and in addition to my school education, I began discovering Arabic literature by myself at home, which made my mother and father proud. My mother helped me set up my own library at home, which included the complete works of Taha Hussein, Tawfiq al-Hakim and Abbas al-Aqqad. From the age of ten, my father constantly gave me old Arabic texts to memorise, such as the poem "Lamiyat al-Ajam", which he explained to me gradually and made me learn by heart in exchange for extra pocket money. The favourite subjects for discussion in our household were culture and books. Then my father became fascinated by space and started grinding a telescope lens by hand – the first made in the Middle East. He then wrote a book called *The Convex Universe* on Einstein's theory of relativity, a quantum leap in scientific books published in Arabic.

Our favourite games, the ones that brought us together as a family, involved swapping poetry puzzles and scientific theories, especially ones to do with space, and intellectual sparring with people visiting the house or my father's surgery, where people came specially from other towns to see the stars and the planets from the roof of the house. We also listened to records of classical music, of which my father had a large collection, and went to the cinema, usually every week, to see two films with a single ticket.

Later the pleasure of painting came into our lives. My father started painting in oils, my mother followed suit, and I joined in too. When I went to university I assumed I would be an artist or a film actress one way or another because that was what I loved most. I had already had some of my writings published in newspapers under pseudonyms when I was twelve, without telling anyone but my mother. All these pastimes and activities took place in a very small house attached to the surgery, as the family budget went towards paying off the debts that arose from my father's repeated political detentions, although he wasn't partisan. He was a patriot who put his nationalism into practice by treating poor people who came from the big refugee camps around Jericho. He treated them, gave them medicine for free, and checked up on them kind-heartedly. His clinic had been the first to open in the town. He supported the nationalist movements and parties, and was even a parliamentary candidate for one party at one time. He was helped by my mother, a women's leader who was an extraordinary and unforgettable principal in UNRWA schools who played a prominent role in nationalist demonstrations and in protests by the prisoners' wives when my father was in prison from time to time.

Sometimes we lived in abject or ordinary poverty, and at other times we lived in luxury. But the cinema, books and art never ceased to be part of our lives. We – my mother and father and I – even invented new ways to use our imaginations: through decorative embroidery in riotous colours, or romantic oil paintings, or through preparing wall magazines for the school, for which my father provided me with scientific information and reports on advances in medicine.

Reading began as a "wonderland" and later this magical antidote became an important part of my life, helping to sweep aside the brutality, torment and homesickness that no human being deserves. With magical words we dress the wounds in our souls, and persuade ourselves to accept our lives. Everything becomes a form of reading.

Republican

25 Cents

WAR ENDS—TOTAL ISRAEL VICTORY

Syrians Collapse In Final Campaign: UN Session Called

U. S. Pilots Hit Power Complex

Resignation of Vance Stirs Up Washington

Ladybird Guest At Clambake

You read a film visually, and the visual arts and music also tell you their story. Everything in the world becomes a story, with subtle variations such as the ones conferred by differences in DNA.

At school I had an Arabic language teacher who made an impression on her classes by bringing important novels from home and lending them to her pupils.

All that came to an end after the tragedy of 1967, or what is known as the Six Day War, which we didn't see as a war but an eviction that turned us into refugees purely by chance. One day my father decided to make a short visit to Amman and leave us, his daughters, with a family of friends: he was working non-stop in the government hospital and couldn't look after us during his long absences from home. My mother had died early, leaving me, the elder sister, to look after four girls.

My father, who believed the Arab regimes' lies about a resounding victory, said we only needed to take a bag with our night-clothes because we would be back within days. But I noticed the book *The Land of Sad Oranges*, which I was reading, on the table, and then caught sight of the orange trees through the window, and a sudden premonition of sadness came over me, so I took with me a picture of my mother, a fountain pen that I treasured and a bar of Nablus soap. The picture reminded me of my mother, the most beautiful part of our family, and the smell of the soap brought back memories of home.

The Arabic cover of The Land of Sad Oranges *by Ghassan Kanafani*

My father was unable to go back to Palestine because on the same day he decided to drive back the only bridge

Adel Fakhouri

between the West Bank and Jordan was blown up, and then he realised that we had become permanent refugees. The journey out of Jericho had been long and arduous. Instead of just one hour for the hundred kilometres, it had taken us six hours, sometimes hiding by the side of the road or in ditches because of the fighter planes and the napalm and the dozens of dead bodies thrown to the side of the road. The whole of my life amounts to very little compared with my memory of that moment when I left home. All of this was done in order to reduce the number of people in the West Bank. They blew up the bridge to prevent us all from going back to our safe homes and happy families that we had left behind, along with our books and paintings. Some of us lost our families, our relatives, our friends, and the skies and trees that we knew. In a single moment we were deprived of everything a person can possess, to end up as just refugees dispersed in many countries.

Later, when I went to university, my head was filled with big dreams of studying something to do with space science, but since no Arab university was teaching such a course I studied philosophy instead. Through universal ideas, I wanted to find out about my own identity and other contrasting identities. There were some prominent names among my professors, such as Sadeq Jalal al-Azem, Adel Fakhouri and Fouad Zakaria. Later, when I moved to the Lebanese

University, I studied psychology under distinguished professors such as Nazzar al-Zain and Mustafa Hejazi. Books continued to throw light on new paths that hadn't occurred to me.

While I was doing my Master's in psychology, and after I had done the written exams and had to complete my dissertation, Beirut went through a frightening period of war, which reached its peak at the end of the 1970s, forcing many people to reduce their activities because it was so difficult to move around. At that time I wrote my first novel, *A Compass for the Sunflower*, about politics, exile and being a refugee. When the novel was well received, I stopped writing my Master's dissertation and started studying English literature. I wanted to read world literature closely so that in my literary choices I wouldn't need to depend on translations. It seemed I was destined for novels at the time, and resuming university studies in a new subject didn't look like an easy option: it was a complex and revolutionary step at the time for me, both as a journalist overburdened with assignments and as a mother to two children trying to survive a terrible war without any help. As part of my studies I had to read thousands of pages of books in English. I carried out this task with great pride and diligence, full of thanks for this choice because of the beauty and splendour of what I was studying. Once I was so engrossed in Shakespeare's sonnets that I wrote one of my own. I then started translating excerpts from international stories for publication in newspapers.

A horrible thing happened to me at that time, when the final draft of my second collection of short stories was sitting in Dar al-Awda publishing house on Corniche al-Mazraa, in the same building as the PLO. When the Israeli army entered Beirut it confiscated the draft, along with other manuscripts from the publishing house. I didn't have any other drafts for several of the stories and so publication of the collection was cancelled. I then wrote other collections of stories that were published later while I was living in Damascus, such as *A*

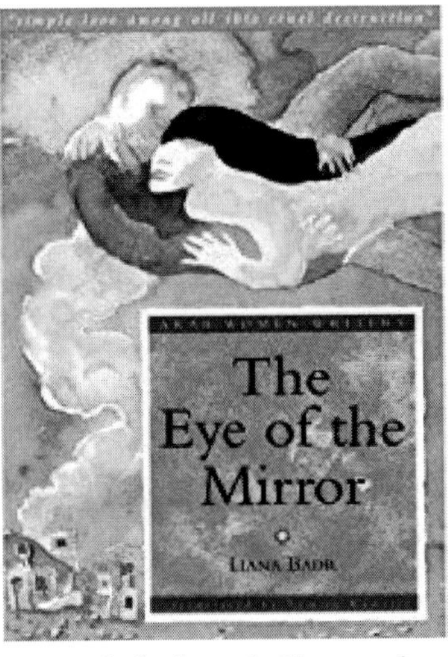

Balcony Over the Fakihani, which was a collection of novellas, *I Want the Daytime* and *Stories of Love and Pursuit*, and was published in Yemen on the initiative of Saadi Youssef.

After the repeated destruction of Palestinian camps in Lebanon, I felt completely psychologically devastated that refugees should face such a bitter fate so far from their homeland. I carried out a sociological, historical and personal study on Tel al-Zaatar, as the first part of a narrative project on the Palestinian presence in Lebanon. But the material was so rich and the events in the camps so momentous that the project evolved into *The Eye of the Mirror*, which combined themes of place, people, stories and the sorrows created by war. So I postponed completing my project on Palestinians in Lebanon and worked on *The Stars of Jericho*, a story suggested to me by the First Gulf War when I saw the horrors inflicted on the Iraqis and the devastation of their lives. I realised that the Arab world was divided forever, and I felt an urge to think back to the Jericho I had lost and our lives there that were suddenly curtailed, though I knew that my account would be like a circle with an enormous hole in the middle – our years in exile from our country.

Later when I was living in Tunis I wrote *Hell of Gold*, a collection of stories about the constant succession of places of refuge that Palestinians have experienced.

My profession as a journalist was the most important factor pushing me into the public sphere: I had to see, hear and learn. My view was that persistence was the quality that novelists needed most. I wrote my first novel in two years, and when a publisher read it and told me it was "excellent material for a novel", I laboured another

Al-Khaima al-Baida'a (The White Tent), *the last novel of Liana Badr was reviewed in* Banipal 58, 2017

year rewriting it. When I wrote *The Eye of the Mirror* I carried out dozens of interviews with witnesses and drew maps of the movements of the characters in the novel. I checked all the details, even down to which nights were moonlit and which were not during the events in the novel. I also tried to gather all the written or oral documentation. I checked all the details of the events so that the characters' backgrounds should have an ambiance that was rich and full of the smell of human beings, despite the wars that exterminate them. I wanted to build the destroyed camp out of words and recover the histories of ordinary people, unlike those imagined in novels with great heroes.

In my last novel, *The White Tent*, I worked for five years to explain the ambiguity in Palestinians' conceptions of things, and in it I asked questions about many things: was the revolution still a revolution? Were romantic heroes still leading us to freedom and justice, or might what was happening be completely different from what was originally intended? I think I worked on the meaning of ambiguity because it represents my character: when people expect me to submit to reality, I'm rebellious, and when they think I'm sure of something, I announce that I don't know anything. I'm a woman from an old world where people were imprisoned because they disagreed, but I was proud of disagreement and defended it. What made me anxious was submission. I don't want to be a carbon copy of what women here and in the wider world aspire to be.

The most important thing I can do is learn to listen to people and their stories, because this is what unites us. I lived in Beirut for ten years, and it was a rich place of learning where the Palestinian resistance movement encountered Lebanese modernity, giving rise to a distinctive cultural hybrid. In Damascus I discovered the history of the ancient East in museums that still smelled of the Ebla and Mari Empires. There I learned how to analyse films, and I identified with

Mahmoud Darwish

Sadiq Jalal al-Azm

the way films rebel and refuse to submit to dictates imposed by fossilised Arab regimes.

I'm indebted to Tunis for giving me a chance for calm reflection, as well as for the warmth of its people and their beautiful compassion for Palestinians. There I learned to devote time to beauty and to make communion with nature a daily objective that would never slip my mind. If I am indebted to anyone's influence, it would be to my philosophy professor Sadiq Jalal al-Azm, who watched over a whole generation with his critical tone, and to writers who criticised the state of the Arab world and tried to lay it bare, such as Sonallah Ibrahim, Zakaria Tamer, Gamal el-Ghitani, and Khalida Said. I am also indebted to all those with whom I had invaluable encounters over many years and who gave me a part of themselves. I learned from every artist, writer or intellectual I met, and make special mention of my great teacher Mahmoud Darwish, who gave me a complete education in aesthetics and humanity.

When I look back at my work – four novels, a collection of novellas, four collections of short stories, three books of poems, a book about Mahmoud Darwish, a book about Fadwa Tuqan, scripts for several films and seven documentary films that I wrote and directed and that won international prizes, I feel this represents only a quarter of what I could have produced if I hadn't had to put up with all these wars, and live under the yoke of this long occupation.

All I want to do is write.

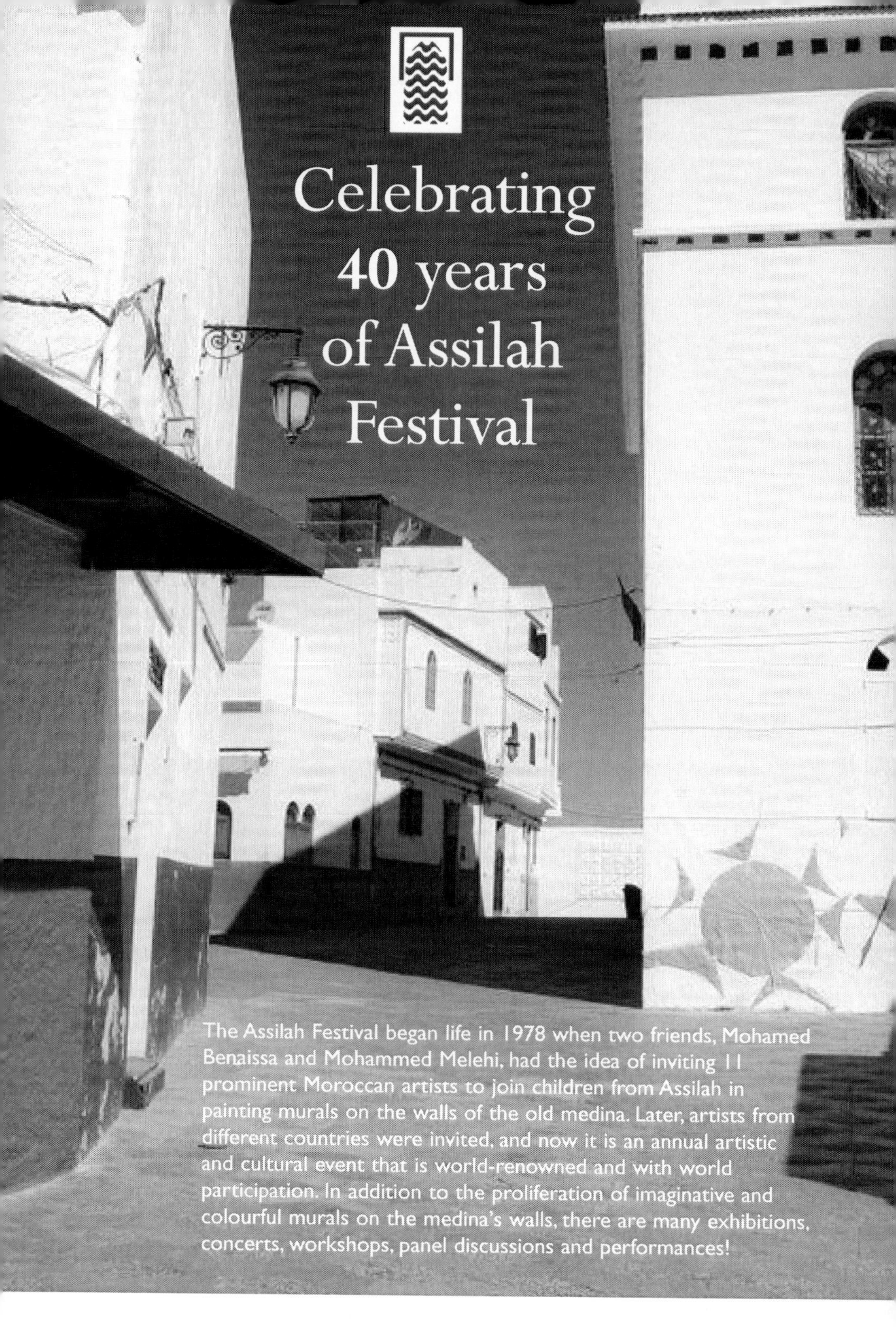

Celebrating 40 years of Assilah Festival

The Assilah Festival began life in 1978 when two friends, Mohamed Benaissa and Mohammed Melehi, had the idea of inviting 11 prominent Moroccan artists to join children from Assilah in painting murals on the walls of the old medina. Later, artists from different countries were invited, and now it is an annual artistic and cultural event that is world-renowned and with world participation. In addition to the proliferation of imaginative and colourful murals on the medina's walls, there are many exhibitions, concerts, workshops, panel discussions and performances!

MARGARET OBANK

Assilah: colours, sounds, and inspiration

I knew about the Assilah Forum Festival for a number of years before going there for the first time in the early years of the new century.

Mohamed Benaissa, who served as both Morocco's Foreign Minister and Minister of Culture, has created, seemingly effortlessly, a month-long annual cultural extravaganza where as many walls of the old medina as possible are elaborately painted and decorated, and all kinds of artistic and cultural expression take place. Invited artists from all over the world, children and students from the town, join various arts workshops, including a print-making one, set up in and around the restored Raissouni Palace, the Palace of Culture, and play their part painting the town. Alongside them run concerts, performances, receptions, a series of 1, 2 and 3-day conferences on different subjects, special debates and panels, most of which include simultaneous translation facilities. There is always an interesting art exhibition in the Hassan II Culture Centre, where many of the conferences and discussions take place and which is graced with a welcoming courtyard for networking between sessions – and a cooling refreshment.

I was immediately impressed, when I first attended the festival, by its friendly, peaceful and relaxed atmosphere. It is a unique international meeting-point, where I have personally met authors, artists, diplomats, journalists, translators, musicians, actors, film directors at a variety of venues, and attended a myriad of cultural events, all of which build on humanity's common features, creating longed-for cultural dialogue and exchange. It was striking to watch flamenco performances in the Raissouni Palace, and imagine that one day the close neighbours of Morocco and Spain will iron out their differences.

Margaret Obank with Mohamed Benaissa, Assilah 2007

Every time I go to Assilah there are new developments in the town. There is now a state of the art public library and conference hall, and I was privileged to attend the opening of two beautiful memorial gardens, one for Mahmoud Darwish following his death in August 2008, and one for Tayeb Salih, who died the following February. I was thrilled to find, at the entrance to the medina, a small garden dedicated to the Iraqi poet Buland al-Haydari. It was initially a strange feeling to be walking in gardens dedicated to the memory of these three artists whom I knew personally. Now I look forward to visiting the gardens, breathing their calm air, and seeing how the plants and trees are growing.

Mohamed Benaissa not only established this month of diverse cultural performance and dialogue, but added to it literary awards for fiction and poetry – the Mohamed Zafzaf Award for the novel, and the Buland al-Haydari Award for a Young Poet, to foster and recognise the central place of creative writing in human society. The finale of each festival also includes awards to citizens of Assilah – from young schoolchildren, to mothers, fathers, workers and pensioners.

It was entirely fitting that Mohamed Benaissa's ceaseless work to develop intercultural dialogue, exchange and creativity was recognised by the Sheikh Zayed Book Award when he was presented with their Cultural Personality of the Year award in 2008.

Last year, 20 July, he oversaw a wonderful day of discussions, with specially invited international panellists, as a celebration of Banipal magazine's 20th year of publication. What a day for dialogue! Thank you, Mohamed Benaissa.

I am thrilled to be a part, this year, of celebrating 40 years of Assilah Forum Festival, 40 years of Mohamed Benaissa's dedication to bringing people together, and to expanding with fresh insight the avenues of creativity and cultural exchange.

ABDUL WAHAB BADRAKHAN

Assilah and Mohamed Benaissa: A Story of Cultural Passion

I can't imagine not having Assilah in my mind and heart. This enchanting historic Moroccan city isn't one which you set out to find. Instead, it's a place to which you're led by chance, and where you remain even after you've left. Nor can I imagine what course my thinking would have taken without Mohamed Benaissa, mayor of Assilah and founder of its renowned annual festival, the Cultural Moussem of Assilah. Benaissa may or may not be aware of the position of esteem in which I hold him. Nevertheless, he has for many years served as a very real source of insight and inspiration for me.

I was there for Assilah's very first cultural festival, or Moussem, forty years ago, and I must confess that at first I was taken aback by what I saw. My initial impression of it was one of pretence, affectation, and illusion. I didn't feel the location was appropriate for what its organisers wanted to achieve: it did not seem to me a venue conducive to meaningful discussion of weighty intellectual issues. Having little grasp of the context, I didn't know what had led up to it, or where it might lead. I had no idea how or why this or that mural had ended up on this or that wall of the city, who it was who had brought together such a motley collection of Arab and non-Arab artists, thinkers, intellectuals, poets and authors. I went away with the impression that the festival's inauguration was basically a nondescript Moroccan town's way of trying to put itself on the world map.

On my flight back to Paris, where I was living at the time, a dear Tunisian friend of mine, Hamadi Essid (1939-1991), a writer and diplomat, launched into a lively commentary on what we had just

Abdul Wahab Badrakhan and Mohamed Benaissa in Assilah

witnessed. According to him, this simple little town had a beautiful future ahead of it. Essid was more informed than I was, and had a keen appreciation for Mohamed Benaissa's courage and the boldness it had taken to start from scratch the way he had, but with love, determination, and a guiding vision that would give him staying power over the long haul. His first step had paved the way for huge strides to come. Admitting that he envied Benaissa for his "dream", which is how he described the Moussem, Essid told me he expected it to be a huge and lasting success, as its instigator had approached the idea not only with passion, but also with organisational skills and a concrete agenda. He also confessed to having had a similar dream of his own once, though various things had got in the way of achieving this. The last thing he said was: "It isn't every day that you meet a politician who's willing to devote this kind of time, effort, expertise and money to a little coastal town that nobody's ever heard of. But it's going to end up with horizons broader than the sea itself, and the scope of its vision will be a gift to future generations."

Sadly, Hamadi Essid didn't live to see Assilah as we see it now, flourishing and growing from one year to the next, gradually being

One of the many different events held in the Raissouni Palace, Assilah

beautified by Benaissa's loving touches and taking on the qualities of his dream. The obsolete building where the Moussem's first discussions took place with the late Muhammad Arkoun, Adonis, Ahmed Abdel Muti Hijazi and others has been transformed into a palace of culture and an ornate work of art in Morocco's distinctive style. Two other unique architectural structures grace Assilah's modest skyline. We saw one of them, the Hassan II International Forum Centre, being built from the ground up. As for the other, it appeared to spring up out of nowhere, and before we knew it it was the Prince Bandar Bin Sultan Library. Still more importantly, and thanks in large part to the Moussem's influence, the townsfolk have taken an increasing interest in the appearance of their houses and the general well-being of the city, from the cleanliness of their streets and neighbourhoods and the flowers in their gardens to their children, who now seek knowledge and dream of a brighter future. Al-Sayd did not live to see the tourists that now flock to the city, having heard about this place that drinks from the well of its deeply rooted past and which, in so doing, has acquired a modernity brimming with future potential. And it all began with the most simple yet brilliant of ideas, and a great deal of aspiration.

This is development as understood and implemented by Mohamed Benaissa. When presented in books and reports, development rarely assigns culture the priority it deserves. Culture is the "forgotten dimension" missing from most developmental initiatives, including not only those that flounder due to insufficient resources, but even those that are otherwise deemed "successful". The reason for this is that in order for people to become genuinely involved and invested in development by making it part of their way of life, it has to be representative of their most authentic cultural values and mores. Benaissa for one never tires of stressing that culture is one of the cornerstones of sustainable development. He has done his utmost to ensure that the Moussem remains faithful to the principle on which it was founded, namely, that culture is Assilah's main source of wealth. To this end, he works tirelessly to encourage the town's residents – with a special emphasis on its young people – to cultivate knowledge in all its facets, from its modernist dimensions to its folkloric treasures. Mohamed Benaissa didn't wait for the early Moussems to prove themselves a success before working to institutionalise his project. From the outset, the Moussem formed part of an institution, namely,

Tchicaya U Tam'si (1931-1988),

the al-Mu'tamid Bin Abbad Summer University. Upon careful reflection, it becomes clear that his choice of name for this institution was no mere coincidence or flight of fancy. Rather, it was a tribute to the last of the Andalusian monarchs of Bani Abbad and to the spirit of renewal and prosperity, the traces of which still linger in abundance in present-day Seville. Al-Mu'tamid is remembered for his love of poetry and the honour he bestowed upon poets from among the common folk of Andalusia, Africa, and Sicily before being deposed and exiled in 1091 CE to Aghmat, Morocco, where he spent the rest of his life.

Since its inception, the Moussem has reserved a special place for poetry, which has always figured prominently in its gatherings. Among the poets celebrated by the Moussem is the Congolese Tchicaya U Tam'si (1931-1988), whose eloquence and penetrating sense of universality have been immortalised through an award bestowed in his name every two years upon a deserving African poet. Another author similarly immortalised is the highly perceptive Iraqi poet Buland al-Haydari (1926-1996). However, given the variety of literary tastes now recognised in the Arab world and the rise of the novel in particular, the Moussem also created a prize for the Arabic novel, which it named after the beloved Moroccan author Mohamed Zafzaf (1945-2001). In so doing, the Moussem has lived up to the versatile spirit that has always been its hallmark, and which is reflected in both its continuously updated activities and events, and the way in which it incorporates and embraces current affairs.

On various occasions and in various countries over the years, I've crossed paths with people with whom I've attended one of Assilah's annual festivals. The days we spent together in that atmosphere of warmth and mutuality seems to have created a bond between us so that when we see each other in a different context, we share a sense of camaraderie, the feeling of belonging to a secret or privileged club of sorts. Indeed, Assilah gave birth to many a long-time friendship that I cherish beyond words. And beyond those who have be-

come friends are countless others, whose names I only wish I could recall, who have been drawn to Assilah from places as diverse as the United States, Latin America, Africa, Europe and the Arab world and who, though I've never met since, left an indelible impression on me. They passed like milestones as the Moussem continued on its journey, from the time when Assilans simply wanted to encounter Westerners and strike up a conversation with them, to the time when they started carving out a niche for their African neighbours, to their endeavours to strengthen their ties with fellow Arabs (whether from their home countries or elsewhere), for whom Assilah had become an indispensable way station.

Since the Moussems began forty years ago, each edition has had a primary theme designed to encourage participants to think about and engage with a particular topic or concern. It is therefore not surprising that successive Moussems have placed every issue imaginable under the microscope: the state, religion and the state, reform of all sorts, education, development, culture, immigration, Arabs and the West, and so on. With the dawn of the new millennium, encounters among the world's civilisations with their inevitable conflicts and conversations have brought the problems of extremism and terrorism to the fore. As new horizons open up for the media, the Moussem has featured numerous reviews of the technological and digital shifts taking place in the field of communications. When several Arab countries witnessed simultaneous popular uprisings, the Moussem grappled unhesitatingly with the questions and concerns raised by this movement. And with the recent resurgence of nationalist bigotries and populist trends in the West, their echoes have been heard in the discussions taking place in Assilah. Nor has the Moussem neglected the changes taking place in Morocco itself. On the contrary, over the decades it has served as an open forum for many of the debates distinct to the country. All of this reflects the diversity of the Moussems' participants and their respective ideas. However, there is a particular person whose presence has been indispensable for modulating, and moderating, the tone of these encounters: that person is Mohamed Benaissa.

By virtue of their specialisations and interests, the people who flock from near and far to Assilah every year are in touch with the developments that become the themes of the Moussem's seminars. But, one may ask, are these issues of any concern to Assilah's locals?

Photo: Margaret Obank

Signs in Arabic, French, English & Spanish in the Buland al-Haydari Garden, Assilah, 2017.

A fair number of cynical comments have been made on this subject, though often out of shortsightedness. Some people think of summer as the time for entertainment festivals that leave behind nothing of substance. But year after year, the Moussem in Assilah has shown itself to belong to a class of its own, leaving an impression on an entire generation of Assilans. If, as a visitor, you take the time to listen to the young women and men who attend or help organise events, you cannot help but sense their pride in what they experience through the Moussem. Seeing the way this initiative enriches their lives and broadens their horizons, they wish the festival would last longer than it does, not because it gives them something to do over the holidays, but because of all they gain from it. A young woman from Assilah told me that if it weren't for the Moussem, she wouldn't have had the chance to listen to Moroccan and other North African musical groups, a Kuwaiti opera troupe, or poets (both men and women) from the UAE and Bahrain. And as I was told by a young man who's a native of the town but who lives away as a student, he comes home every summer anxious to find out what Benaissa has in store for him. "He surprises us every time," the young man said. "One Moussem, for example, there were musical performances from Morocco, Burkina Faso, Ghana, India, Italy, Austria, Portugal, and Spain."

Whether they realise it or not, these young people come away from Assilah with changed minds and hearts. Even the city looks different to them from how it did before. Their eyes are opened to parks named after great souls – the likes of Mahmoud Darwish, Tayeb Salih,

Mohammed Aziz Lahbabi, and Tchicaya U Tam'si. They see celebrities from all over the world, some of whom they were already familiar with and others they've come to know for the first time, walking down the streets and mixing with the people of Assilah. They've been with Benaissa as he invites them to take pictures, or steals a moment here or there to remind children and adults alike to keep the streets clean. This detail, however seemingly trivial, has a profound impact. In fact, some Assilans complain that it's the foreigners who litter the town, throwing their rubbish every which way. Be that as it may, a prize is awarded at the close of each Moussem for the cleanest street, or for the house with the most artfully decorated entrance. But the most poignant moments of all are those when, for example, a widowed mother is rewarded for her heroic struggle and sacrifice to raise and educate her children, who have now risen to positions of note. Or when the prize is awarded to an ageing fisherman, or an athlete, or a student. It is gestures of loyalty, gratitude and appreciation such as these that come to symbolise the success of each Moussem , and without which no Moussem would be complete.

When Benaissa refers to the Assilah Moussem as "a cultural project", he means it. The project is also intensely personal to him: an edifice he has built brick by brick, acutely aware of what makes it unique and at the same time universal. He has contributed profoundly to the Moussem's every detail, with ideas he has gleaned from the experiences of others, from his travels far and wide, and from other experiences in his own life. Most importantly, however, he considers the endeavour still to be incomplete, and strives constantly to incorporate new elements into its programme. Mohamed Benaissa is a role model for both his own generation and for generations to come, an inspiration to all who seek meaningful and constructive change, and a living reminder that whoever invests in culture has nothing to fear from the vicissitudes of Time.

Translated by Nancy Roberts

Abdul Wahab Badrakhan is a Lebanese political analyst and journalist.

CHÉRIF KHAZNADAR

Forty years of love and tolerance

I am, without a doubt, one of the first foreign guests of the Moussem of Assilah, one who has participated in more than thirty of the annual festivals.

I came to know Assilah when we were all, the guests that is, accommodated in Al-Khaima, a small hotel outside the city, and we had to walk in the sand to reach the Raissouni Palace and the painted old city walls. They were the emblem, the hallmark of a truly unique cultural festival, unique because it combined everything that elsewhere was presented separately: shows, conferences, seminars, exhibitions, workshops . . . In a few days those who had the privilege of knowing the existence of this Moussem could plunge into the waters of international culture. The festival was experienced as a precious moment of privilege, outside time and space, a rejuvenating experience.

In a book entitled *Assilah, Culture and the City* I told the story of the extraordinary adventure of the birth and growth of this event, which has been long cited as an example of the role culture can play in transforming a poor little fishing village into a prosperous city, rich in not only cultural but also in social, touristic, and commercial structures. It is an example of what culture could do to place a city on the coveted map of the artistic and cultural world.

On the occasion of the fortieth anniversary of the Cultural Moussem of Assilah, it is necessary to do justice to those who "made" this Moussem by naming all of them: its first creators, its volunteer organisers, and its participants – artists, intellectuals, journalists, politicians, etc. An impressive list which alone would fill a book, a list in the memory of the man who has "carried" this exceptional festival and who knew how to gather around him the teams who have been its backbone: Mohamed Benaissa.

Benaissa, as we say in Morocco where a person's first name, except

Chérif Khaznadar

for kings, is little or not mentioned, has performed miracles of tenacity, endurance and courage, with the will to realise his dream and share it with generations of children from his city, and intellectuals from the Arab world and elsewhere. To pay tribute to him is to pay homage to all those who believed in him, who supported him with their friendship, their presence, and their memories. Many have since left us, but their names remain engraved in the stones of the streets, the monuments, and the events that Benaissa dedicated to them, for he is also a sentimental soul. He hides this carefully, but in my eyes it is his most important quality as without it nothing would have been possible. This quality, together with his love for his city, for the Zelisi locals, for his family, his friends, and his country has made the impossible possible.

Forty years of happiness in the celebration of culture and its creators is a birthday that is celebrated with joy. Happy birthday Assilah, happy birthday Benaissa.

Translated from the French by Ghada Mourad

Chérif Khaznadar is a French poet, novelist and director, of Syrian origin. He is president of the House of World Cultures in Paris

MIGUEL ÁNGEL MORATINOS

The Assilah Festival: Culture and Art for Development

Forty years ago my good friend Mohamed Benaissa had the splendid idea of organising a festival of culture and art in his city, Assilah, to bring into relief the history, present and future of this small locality in northern Morocco.

Thus, in 1978 Mohamed Benaissa took what was a bold and risky wager. We imagine that when they embarked on the project, various questions must have been asked: Why not use culture and art as an engine of development and progress? Why not make something extremely "useful" out of what is "useless", as Nuccio Ordine, the great Italian thinker, would say? Why not turn a modest place in northern Morocco into a vital point of encounter if one wants to observe "modernity" and the ways in which a new era is evolving?

All these questions received positive answers and this innovative initiative was born. Neither Morocco nor the Mediterranean area possessed a project that aimed to bring together art and the creative spirit as an engine for the socio-economic development of an entire region. Ever since, this city's medina has become for several days each year an interactive space for sociable encounters and cultural exchange.

Painting was one of the first dimensions chosen by Benaissa and his team; the city would be transformed via artistic expression. Initially, they invited a group of artistic friends to paint the walls of the medina together with the city's inhabitants with a view to revitalising tourism and promoting interaction between citizens in the urban space. Later, alongside the striking murals exhibited in Assilah's narrow streets, they gradually added new elements to the simple mural exhibition, such as cultural dialogues and artistic get-togethers.

Intellectual debate, art and thought were incorporated into sum-

Miguel Ángel Moratinos speaking at last year's Assilah Festival

mery days that attracted artists and audiences from both sides of the Mediterranean.

At the time our friend Benaissa was Minister of Culture in the government of King Hassan II. He would soon be given new responsibilities at a national and international level, and foreign affairs naturally led him to use the cultural diplomacy of his city to present his country to the Mediterranean region, to the African continent, and the world.

My links to the festival go back a long time though they are really quite recent if we consider how long the festival has existed. It was in my first year as Spain's Minister for Foreign Affairs in 2004 that I first participated. That was a year of renewed entente and reconciliation between Morocco and Spain, and Minister Benaissa thoroughly grasped the natural desire of our two peoples to re-activate bonds of cooperation and friendship.

His invitation was a success, the people of Assilah gave me a friendly welcome, and I tried to return their gesture with the same respect and affection with which they received me. From 2004 to today I have always returned to Assilah. My presence there over thirteen years has allowed me to watch the festival develop. The Assilah Festival has continually embraced fresh initiatives. As well as art and

Assilah is always a source of inspiration and knowledge. There I became familiar with the awakening of the African continent

culture, every year the festival devotes wide-ranging sessions to debating the big issues of the day, in an international, multidisciplinary context. The array of subjects is impressive and that, in itself, expresses the clear vision Benaissa and his team had, and still have, of the big changes the world and the whole Mediterranean region are experiencing. The most sensitive issues have been on the agenda: immigration, refugees, terrorism or the political crises arising from the Arab Spring, as well as the permanent instability in the Middle East. Moreover, there have been frank discussions of the crisis in Europe, the future of the Mediterranean, and the big political debates at a world level: democracy and populism, energy challenges, the Objectives of Sustainable Development or the problems related to the clash of cultures and civilisations. In effect, all the questions that affect and will affect our common future

For me, Assilah is always a source of inspiration and knowledge. There I became familiar with the awakening of the African continent. It enabled me to establish contact with leaders and key politicians on the continent, thus facilitating my work as a diplomat and negotiator when later I dealt with some of the contentious issues that are difficult to resolve in that part of the world. I would like to affirm,

At the Assilah Festival in 2007, Abdou Diouf, President of Senegal 1981–2000 (l), and Kofi Annan, Secretary-General of the United Nations 1997–2006.

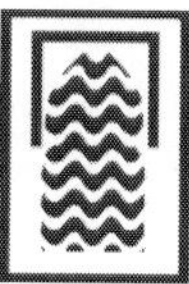

Benaissa and Moratinos at the Hassan II Centre for International Culture, Assilah

quite unambiguously, that the festival in Assilah enjoys much better credentials than Davos; the spirit that imbues the intellectual exchanges, the freedom of expression, the framework of mutual respect and openness is something hard to find at other conferences of this nature. Assilah deserves recognition for its excellent intellectual level and because it is one of the few forums where leading players from every continent can freely debate the future of humanity. Africans, Arabs, Latin Americans and Asians meet in this small locality on the frontiers of Europe to show that mutual respect is possible in the twenty-first century, and that it is possible to fulfil the aim of creating that alliance of civilisations and cultures some still think is a mere utopia.

So, congratulations for 40 years of excellent work and dedication to peace and understanding between the peoples and nations of the whole of humanity. We hope that the festival will continue to defend these essential values where art, culture and thought prevail over short-term gains and that, where what might have initially seemed "useless" has become a useful, wholly successful necessity.

Thank you, Assilah, and thank you, Mohamed Benaissa, for all these years of cultural enrichment.

Translated from the Spanish by Peter Bush

Miguel Ángel Moratinos was Spain's Minister for Foreign Affairs and Cooperation, 2004–2010

RUDRONEEL GHOSH

Assilah: Morocco's bridge to the world

There's no denying the fact that we are in the throes of a great global transition. The world as we know it is dramatically changing. And while change isn't new, what is leading to the social, economic and political turbulence is the quantum leap of change with which we are faced. Driven by radical technological advances – often beyond the grasp of the ordinary mind – these changes are fundamentally altering the way in which we live and relate to each other. The pockets of chaos in the world today are in fact a reflection of the old brushing up against the new. And when the dust settles, we will be ushered into a new world system.

What will this new world system look like? The tide of technological advancement has already altered the way we communicate, work and express ourselves. The next wave will witness the advent of Artificial Intelligence (AI) permeating every aspect of life. This has raised the prospect of humanity receding, as machines begin dominating labour. But can humanity truly recede? Can machines come to rule the world? Can robots create a new 'civilisation'? I disagree. Humanity is integral to civilisation. But in an AI-driven world, humanity once again would have to adapt.

Which is why I say that the future belongs to the economy of ideas. With production processes increasingly being automated, ideas will become the new currency, the new gold reserve, and the new oil. Countries that invest in human resources today will reap the most benefits tomorrow. The population, armed forces or natural resources of nations will matter far less than their ability to produce new ideas for the world and enrich humanity. In fact, I believe that we are likely to chance upon a future where artists, in-

Rudroneel Ghosh

tellectuals and philosophers will regain the status they enjoyed at the height of the ancient Greek states, or at the zenith of the Mughal empire in medieval India, or at the crest of the European Renaissance. I foresee the coming of a new Renaissance, with machines freeing us up to devote greater energy to intellectual subjects such as art, polity, society and spirituality.

It is against this backdrop that I commend the endeavours of the Assilah Forum Foundation. In its fortieth year now, the forum's aim of providing a platform to the most respected intellectuals, scholars, policymakers, ministers and heads of government – from the Middle East and North Africa region and beyond– to discuss hot-button issues facing the world is truly welcome. For it is a fact that Morocco finds itself in a neighbourhood that has, for various convenient and unjustifiable reasons, been treated in a stepmotherly fashion by the international community. Few in the comity of nations believed that Morocco – a North African country without oil – would have any-

Photo call for children attending a painting workshop at the Assilah Festival

thing significant to contribute to global discourse. How Morocco and the Assilah Forum have proved them wrong!

Morocco has shown the world that one can prosper just through the richness of ideas. Through a spirit of sharing and brotherhood. Through committing to truth and inquiry. Indeed, it is this yearning for knowledge, self-reflection and exchange of ideas that guides the Assilah Forum. And today the world is sitting up and taking note of Morocco and Assilah.

I was privileged to be a part of the forum in 2017, which saw an extraordinary gathering of people from across the world debate the rise of populism, right-wing politics and other allied topics. I thank Minister Mohamed Benaissa from the bottom of my heart for offering up Assilah as a great big banyan tree, under whose shade intellectuals from far and wide have come to drink the nectar of knowledge. I also commend him for turning Assilah into a refuge for artists. Under the aegis of the forum, the hamlet of Assilah has transformed into a kaleidoscope of colours through collaborations between local and foreign artists. This artistic oeuvre is not just an ode to human talent, but also a strong statement of cultural harmony and tradition in the face of obscurantist ideology. It is as if Assilah cries out in one resounding voice: "We will not go into that good night quietly. We will live and fill this beautiful world with more colour."

With respect to both its intellectual and cultural dimensions, the Assilah Forum is truly an oasis for those who care about the world's present health and future status. Additionally, it has emerged as a veritable bridge between Africa – particularly North Africa – and the rest of the world. And in times of chaos and confusion, the wise build bridges. It is no wonder, then, that Morocco's steady emergence as an influential voice within Africa, the Arab world and among the comity of nations is reflected in the Assilah Forum. In fact, I would even venture to suggest that Morocco's rise as an African-Maghrebi influencer is a direct result of the intellectual bedrock that one witnesses at the Assilah Forum.

As the world enters uncharted territories, we need the Assilah Forum to provide direction and facilitate communication. We need the Assilah Forum to debate the future course of humanity. We need the Assilah Forum to help push civilization to the next stage, even as the material world comes to be dominated by machines. And, most importantly, we need the Assilah Forum to provide ideas to policymakers to make the world a better place. And the best ideas are birthed when people and institutions interact, share resources and learn from each other.

Thus, with the world increasingly finding out that many of the things it hitherto valued are increasingly insignificant, we have in Morocco and Assilah an example that investing in human capital pays. And this is what Morocco wishes to share with Africa and the rest of the world. I hope and pray that the Assilah Forum goes from strength to strength and becomes a model for the world in preparation for the oncoming economy of ideas.

As for Assilah and its guardian angel Minister Benaissa, I borrow these words from Robert Frost:

"The woods are lovely, dark and deep,/ But I have promises to keep,/ And miles to go before I sleep,/ And miles to go before I sleep."

Rudroneel Ghosh is a journalist with *The Times of India*, the largest English newspaper in India. As an editorial writer he analyses latest global trends and the nuances of international politics from the perspective of one of the fastest-growing big economies in the world. He is a vocal advocate of India-Morocco relations.

HASSOUNA MOSBAHI

Benaissa and Assilah: A Love Story

The sweetest dreams are those which consume you at an early stage of life, and don't leave you until they come true. The childhood dream of Mohamed Benaissa was to see his hometown, Assilah, a much better place. This dream turned into an obsession when he came to know that the town, nestling on the shore of the Atlantic, had been the home of his family for four centuries.

His adult life saw him travel the world. He spent several years in Cairo, where he had the chance to meet the city's elite, among them writers, poets, and singers whom he had admired as a young boy. However, the most formative period of his life was his stay in the United States, where he was able to "see himself clearly" and "recognize his strengths and weaknesses", and where he met with people who were "at once great and simple."

At first it was quite tough for the young Moroccan, having lived through the agonies of colonialism, to settle into that alien world. For several months he remained entangled in the past, possessed by a strong yearning for his home and traditions. As days passed, however, he realized that he had to undergo his own transformation if he was to succeed in a country that owed its achievements and grandeur to adventurers who had come from all corners of the globe.

On one particularly memorable occasion he was sitting in the student café with Professor Charlie, a lecturer at the College of Journalism and Economics. Benaissa, who had been eating with a knife and fork, was astounded to see that this professor, who had more than twenty publications to his name, was eating with his bare hands, even wiping his lips with his fingers! It was at this moment that, back at his apartment, the perplexed student made up his mind to adopt a much more natural and easygoing manner in his daily life. He dis-

Forum d'Assilah
2016
Forum d'Assilah
2016
Forum d'Assilah
2016
Forum d'Assilah
2016

Mohamed Benaissa presents Tunisian writer Hassouna Mosbahi with the Assilah Festival's Mohamed Zafzaf Prize for the Arabic Novel 2016

carded his fancy suits, ties and shirts for more modest attire and, in so doing, freed himself of many of the complexes which had previously beset him.

During that period, Benaissa also made the acquaintance of a lecturer called Irvin, who had embraced Islam in the city of Tétouan with the help of the late Sheikh Dawood, who owned one of the most prominent bookshops in Morocco. The advice Irvin gave to Benaissa was this: "If you can go home, go and engage in rewriting your country's history, for it has not yet been written." The professor went on to supply Benaissa with important references in various subject areas, granting him crucial insight into his country's social history and, at the same time, a much better understanding of himself.

Benaissa's tours of the world took him to Rome, Ghana, Addis Ababa and many other African cities, where he met with notable political, cultural, and intellectual figures and gained an insight which was to prove invaluable to him when he later became Minister of Culture, and then of Foreign Affairs.

After a twenty-year absence, Mohamed Benaissa finally returned to Assilah in 1977. But an enormous shock awaited him. His birth town had turned into a complete shambles. Its old neighbourhoods resembled huge piles of ruins; the streets and squares had become a permanent dumping ground, and its people lived in isolation from

Moroccan writer Mohamed Choukri, French Foreign Minister Hubert Vedrine, Moroccan painter Mohammed Melehi and Tunisian writer Hassouna Mosbahi, Assilah 2000

the rest of the world. These scenes soon began to haunt him constantly, like one dreadful, never-ending nightmare. Then one night, on his way back from Tangier with his friend, the artist Mohammed Melehi, an idea struck him: how about creating a festival of art and culture to rescue his beloved coastal city from its miserable reality?

He did not have any difficulty selling the idea to his friend; however, the truth was that most Moroccan intellectuals had absolutely no interest in it. It was a time when Morocco was reeling under the so-called "years of lead": scores of progressive and leftist intellectuals were in prison, whilst others had fled for their lives. It was also a period of incredible cultural suffocation. There were no cultural magazines or supplements, or indeed any platforms espousing visions which did not align with the official standpoint of the regime. In such a climate, it was only natural that progressive intellectuals would dismiss Benaissa's project as a pro-regime initiative, or even as an attempt by the regime to camouflage its oppressive policies. For the rest of the intellectuals, most of whom generally shied away from outright opposition and criticism of the regime, the idea sounded utopian, impossible to actualize. They felt Asila lacked the essential infrastructure that would enable it to host a cultural festival of the standard to which he aspired.

Yet for a natural adventurer like Benaissa, none of these presented serious hurdles. Wasting no time, he persevered with his dream project. Of course, he was aware that Assilah was lacking in essential tourist infrastructure. The only hotel in the town was tiny and not exactly luxurious. Yet, embracing the natural and easygoing outlook on life which his time in the US had taught him, he managed to see his project come to fruition. Prominent artists, writers, poets and intellectuals started to flow into Assilah and quickly took to the simplicity of life there, willingly staying in its humble hotels and lamenting the moment when they had to depart. The Italian novelist Alberto Moravia didn't think twice about taking a donkey-pulled cart from the railway station to downtown, and could be seen every morning sitting in the café by the gate of the ancient medina, recording his reflections on a typewriter.

By the start of the 1980s, after only two years, the Assilah Festival had risen to stardom, not only within Morocco but also across the Arab world and Europe. Its distinguished guest list included the French singer Georges Moustaki and the celebrated South African

singer Miriam Makeba, as well as many prominent writers and poets such as Buland al-Haydari, Adonis, Abdel Wahab al-Bayati, Tayeb Salih, Raja'a Al-Naqqash, Ahmed Abdel Muti Hijazi and Tchicaya U Tam'si, among others. A special event was organised in honour of the renowned Senegalese poet Léopold Senghor.

The great efforts made by Mohamed Benaissa to lift his tiny city out of obscurity soon attracted the attention of King Hassan II. The monarch, who had just started to reach out to political parties and other opposition forces, did not hesitate to appoint Benaissa as Minister of Culture, which only added to the lure of the festival at a regional and international level. Today, Assilah plays host to major events and lively debate featuring writers, poets, and intellectuals from the Arab world, Africa, Europe, the United States, and the world over.

The Assilah Festival owes part of its success to the open-door philosophy of Benaissa, who firmly believes that no culture can flourish without interaction and engagement with other cultures, and that secluded cultures will always be at risk of destruction. Being simultaneously part of the Arab world, close to Europe and geographically and historically linked to the African continent, he sees it as incumbent upon Morocco to build bridges with its neighbours, and that it is the political and cultural elite who must shoulder this responsibility.

Another secret behind the success of Assilah is the character of Mohamed Benaissa: highly charismatic, uniquely humane and with a deep and insightful knowledge of the state of affairs not only in his own country, but also around the world. He is also blessed with clarity of vision, candidness, and the ability to confront challenges.

One summer night, as I sat with Benaissa in La Perle restaurant, he spoke at length about his passion for Assilah. Joyful at the realisation of a long-held dream, he started singing Mohamed Abd al-Muttalib's song in his tuneful voice: "I loved you, do love you now and will do forever" – a tribute to his beloved hometown, that he crowned with fame and glory.

Translated by Adil Babikir

Hassouna Mosbahi is a Tunisian novelist, journalist and translator

SAFAR

A LITERARY JOURNEY THROUGH ARAB CINEMA

13-18 SEPTEMBER 2018

NADIA EL-SEBAI

SAFAR
FILM FESTIVAL 2018

This year marks the fourth edition of the Safar Film Festival, the only festival dedicated to Arab cinema in the UK. Presented in collaboration with our longstanding partner the ICA, and for the first time this year, the Institut Français, the festival's mission is to stimulate appreciation and understanding of, as well as international demand for, Arab cinema in all its quality, vibrancy and diversity. In past years, the festival has focused on popular and contemporary cinema; this year, we have chosen to focus on literature and storytelling in cinema, and are delighted to partner with our friends at Banipal on both this complementary issue of the magazine and the festival itself. Dedicated to pushing the boundaries of Arab literature in translation, their work over the past 20 years has been instrumental in raising the profile of Arab arts in the UK. It is our pleasure to join forces and celebrate how literature has inspired and enriched cinema in the Arab world, showcasing a fantastic line-up of both authors and film-makers across our two platforms.

Literature and film have always enjoyed a symbiotic relationship, and adaptations have dominated box offices the world over since the cinema industry came to prevalence in the 20th century. In the Arab world, many of the major motion pictures that first dominated screens 50 years ago were adaptations of pioneering mid-century authors – Naguib Mahfouz, for example, and Ghassan Kanafani – whose names and works are now globally recognised. These adaptations, however, have somewhat disappeared from view. Despite their popularity at the time, and the punch they pack in terms of cultural

history, many of the films from this era have never left the region; some have barely seen the light of day for 20 or so years. Safar 2018 will endeavour to redress this, platforming and in some cases preserving these rare works of cinema, bringing them back into the spotlight alongside their literary counterparts.

This year's Safar thus looks back as well as forward, bringing a wide array of classic Arab cinema from the last 50 years to London audiences alongside contemporary titles also inspired by, or adapted from, works of literature from across the world. We'll be hearing from an assortment of film-makers, scriptwriters, and authors about their art, and also discussing the journey that takes place when a work is adapted: from what is perhaps lost in the translation from one medium to another, to what is gained.

The official programme will be released in August, and this special feature in *Banipal 62* serves to illuminate our literary theme, and stimulate dialogue and thought ahead of the festival. A natural pairing as both Safar and *Banipal* magazine thrive on great stories, and the power of telling them the world over. Join us in September to be part of Safar's story, and explore the depths and diversity of Arab literature and cinema in all its glory.

Nadia El-Sebai is Executive Director of The Arab British Centre

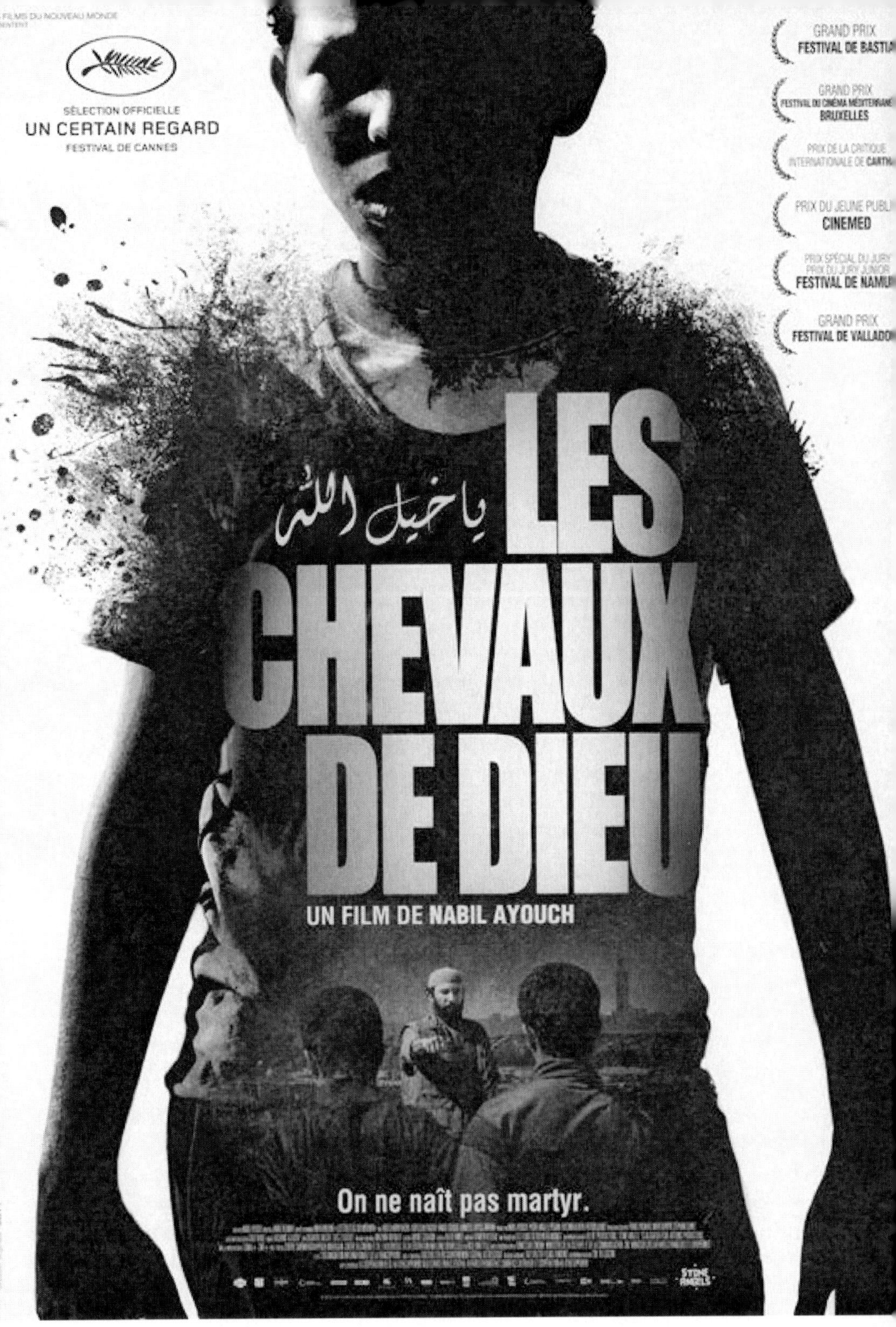
SÉLECTION OFFICIELLE
UN CERTAIN REGARD
FESTIVAL DE CANNES
GRAND PRIX
FESTIVAL DE BASTIA
GRAND PRIX
FESTIVAL DU CINÉMA MÉDITERRANÉ
BRUXELLES
PRIX DE LA CRITIQUE
INTERNATIONALE DE CARTHA
PRIX DU JEUNE PUBLI
CINEMED
PRIX SPÉCIAL DU JURY
PRIX DU JURY JUNIOR
FESTIVAL DE NAMU
GRAND PRIX
FESTIVAL DE VALLADO
يا خيل الله
LES CHEVAUX DE DIEU
UN FILM DE NABIL AYOUCH
On ne naît pas martyr.

JOSEPH FAHIM

Literary adaptations in Arab cinema: The lost chapter

It would not be far-fetched to say that the 21st century has so far been a golden age for Arab literature. Over the past 15 years, a new wave of literature has swept across the region and reignited worldwide interest in the Arabic novel, spearheaded by the phenomenal success of Egyptian Alaa Al-Aswany's *The Yacoubian Building* in 2002. The establishment of the International Prize for Arabic Fiction (also known as the Arabic Booker) five years later was an instant success, contributing in part to the growing number of translations across the globe. As a result, the wealth of writing talent across the region has begun to be recognized more widely, along with the rich literary heritage of the region, and the challenges it has faced.

Arabic literature also flourished in the Islamic Golden Age, from the 8th to the 14th century. After this, a long period of dormancy ensued, with literary output from the region quashed in subsequent centuries by the rampant Ottoman reign and colonial rule. The journey of the Arab world into modern literature was therefore long and uneasy. It's difficult to discern unified literary trends across the region before the 20th century; individual writers in disparate parts of the Middle East came and went, leaving sporadic impact on the cultural life of these countries. Each country would take decades to find its own distinctive literary identity.

National cinemas of the region would take even longer, each embarking on a lengthy, jagged period of gestation, and an even longer maturing phase. More than literature, though, the development of cinema would require affluent economies to set up and nurture the industry, backed by a considerable degree of artistic freedom and education. Thus, development of cinema as an art-form, as a mode of expression, as a language, vastly varied from one country to another.

Nahida al-Rammah and Sami Qaftan in the Iraqi film Al-Dhami'oun (The Thirsties)

The marriage of cinema and literature in the Arab world was not going to be equal, consistent or seamless; but when it worked, it was a revelation. Throughout the Arab world, literature helped cinema discover and foster its national identity, used in part to cast off the shadow of colonisation. Cinema, meanwhile, helped to popularise these indigenous narratives, exploring texts from different angles and shedding light on the innovation these narratives encompassed. Egypt, home of the oldest industry in the region, led the way, thanks to a surge in literary adaptations of some of the country's foremost writers (Naguib Mahfouz, Yusuf Sibai, Taha Hussein and, later, Ihsan Abdel-Quddous) following the abolition of monarchy in 1952. Morocco had sporadic, if copious, attempts at adapting texts for the screen, with the likes of *The Barber of the Poor District*, directed by Mohamed Reggab in 1982; *Zift* (Tayeb Saddiki, 1984) and *Salat al-Gha'ib* (Mohamed Banati, 1995). Syria encouraged filmmakers to adapt a host of novels from across the region during the '70s – the high point of Syrian cinema, resulting in some of the most accomplished Arab films in history, including Tewfik Saleh's *The Dupes* and Bilal al-Sabouni's *The Fifth Castle*. Throughout the years, a number of literary adaptations from Algeria, Tunisia, Palestine, Iraq and Kuwait began to surface. The vast majority were forgotten, while some became iconic works in Arab cinema. Nearly all, however, remain unseen outside of their respective countries, brushed off by international programmers and critics alike.

The film The Search *was adapted from a 1964 novel by Naguib Mahfouz* Al-Tareeq, *the book being translated into English in 1987 by Mohamed Islam, edited by Magdi Wahba, and published by Doubleday in 1991.*

The Safar Film Festival intends to change this reality, offering a programme that highlights one of the most under-explored chapters of Arab film history. The rise in profile of Arab film-makers over the past few years (several Oscar nominations; robust box office receipts; extensive participation in the world's biggest film festivals) has spawned a number of revivals and restorations that demonstrated the unpredictability of the Arab cinematic heritage: a rich, unwieldy canon, constantly defying expectation.

The history of literary adaptations is a reflection not only of Arab cinema in general, but of Arab history. For instance, the surge of literary adaptations in Egypt in the mid '50s came in tandem with the 1952 revolution, and the desire to terminate the cultural influence of Britain and France. It took Algeria even longer to exorcise French colonialist influence, with the first Arabic-language Algerian novel arriving as late as 1971 (Bin Haduqah's *Rih al-Janub*), and which became the source material for one of the first Algerian features. Arabic-writing satirists, such as Ali Douagi, fared better in Tunisia – their influence there was far stronger than in any other Arab nation under occupation. In Palestine, meanwhile, literature was primarily focused on resistance, whether through reviving the memories of the pre-Nakba period, or documenting the physical and emotional repercussions of the Israeli occupation – a function that defined Palestinian cinema of the '90s.

Challenges surrounding finance, censorship, and attitudes towards the preservation of each nation's cinematic heritage also reflect the turbulent state of the region over the past half-century. Following its surge in the early '50s, a radical drop in the number of literary adaptions in Egypt mirrored the larger decline of Egyptian culture in the mid '70s; in Algeria, the one-dimensional histrionics of their war movies darkened in tone as the Civil War began to loom. For Syria, on the other hand, the mid '70s saw a brief period of freedom and economic prosperity which, through the General Organization of Cinema, resulted in the release of some of the most ambitious Arabic films of the 20th century, including a number of remarkable literary adaptations – before it was halted by Hafez al-Assad's increasing repressiveness. *The Dupes*, directed by Tawfik Saleh and based on Ghassan Kanafani's novel *Men in the Sun*, is one of these landmark films, and will be screened as part of the festival, much to our excitement.

Many Arab adaptations share common locales (the countryside in Egyptian Youssef Chahine's *The Land*; Iraqi Mohammed Shokry Gamil's *The Thirsties* and Ahmed Rachedi's *Opium and the Baton*) and common themes (man vs. destiny in Chahine's *The Sixth Day* and Hossam El Din Mostafa's *The Search;* the physical cost of national emancipation in Algerian Selim Riad's *Winds of the South* and Rachedi's *Opium*). Yet the approach, both aesthetic and thematic, is never the same. The post-Nakba quiet despair of Saleh's *The Dupes* is different from Yousri Nasrallah's sweeping *Gate of the Sun*; the manifestations of religious faith in Khalid Al Siddiq's *Wedding of Zein* have little to do with the scepticism of Marwan Hamed's *Lili*.

Taken as a whole, Arab literary adaptations represent a vibrant mosaic, imbued with diverse aesthetic tendencies, narratives and ideas. With the destitute state of archiving in the region, and with the reductive fixation on the new, it is more imperative than ever to frame this forgotten part of Arab film history in an appropriate context, and assert its place in the canon of Arab film.

The Safar Film Festival programme shall thus be a space for discovery, for exploration and for shining an entirely new light on Arab cinema.

The famous actress and singer Dalida (1933–1987) in a scene from Youssef Chahine's film The Sixth Day

Un film de Youssef Chahine
Le Sixième Jour
DALIDA
Mohsen Mohieddine

AMIN ZAOUI

Opium and the Stick: The novel's poetics and the film's ambition

Algerian novelist Mouloud Mammeri (1917-1989) was a controversial intellectual. Bold, rigorous, and candid, he is considered one of the founding fathers of the Algerian novel written in French. Mammeri lived by his principles and died without compromising them. During the Algerian Revolution against French colonisation, he was one of the intellectuals who joined the National Liberation Front. He penned some of the speeches in defence of the Algerian cause at the United Nations General Assembly, delivered by Mhamed Yazid, the then Minister of Information in the provisional government of the Algerian Republic.

Although primarily celebrated for his classic literary works such as *La Colline oubliée* (1952, The Forgotten Hill), *Le Sommeil du juste* (1952, Sleep of the Righteous), and *L'Opium et le bâton* (1965, Opium and the Stick), his contribution to research was no less important. Mammeri was a keen linguist, anthropologist and researcher who wrote up the foundations of Amazigh grammar, and deserved the title of "Sibawayh of the Amazigh language"[1]. His seminal work on the Amazigh language, *Tajerrumt n'tamazight* (Kabyle Grammar) was first published in 1976 (Maspero).

In addition to his writing and research interests, Mammeri was also drawn to the significance of visual media. He believed that films, both documentary and narrative, could capture and communicate cultural, political, and historical messages more powerfully than just the written word. He wrote the scripts for two documentaries *Dawn*

Poster of the film and the book cover

of the Sentenced to Death (1965), directed by Ahmed Rachedi, and *Death of a Long Night* (1979), directed by al-Guthi Bin Ddouch.

After Independence in 1962 Mammeri's literary texts began to appeal to the Algerian movie industry. Two of his major novels were made into films, with *L'Opium et le Bâton* (1970), being the first feature film produced after Independence and based on his novel of the same title. The film was directed by Ahmed Rachedi and produced by the Algerian National Institute of Cinema (ONCIC). Mammeri's other novel made into a movie was *La Colline oubliée* (The Forgotten Hill). Directed by Abderrahmane Bouguermouh (1936–2013), it was the first Algerian feature film in the Amazigh language. The production of the movie took place between 1992 and 1995.

Mammeri's novels are thoroughly visual and rich in descriptions, vividly written with an abundance of fine details of nature and human life, ranging from costumes, topography, landscape, to language and emotions. Artistically, Mammeri is close to naturalism, especially in his understanding of the nature of tribal life in the mountains. His accounts of nature can be described as oil paintings made of words. His morphological and physical portrayals of characters are drawn from the daily lives of simple peasants from the tribal areas, including his own village of Taourirt Mimoun, which was also the birthplace of the distinguished scholar Mohammed Arkoun (1928–2010)

Mammeri's constant highlighting of daily life in the mountain region is not an expression of isolation or negative regionalism. Rather, he was writing the lives of ordinary people who lived in the area where he was born,and in doing that following in the footsteps of fellow novelist Mohammed Dib (1920–2003) who meticulously documented the traditions of disadvantaged families in Tlemcen in his trilogy on Algeria, *La Grande Maison* (1952,The Big House), *L'Incendie* (1954,The Fire) and *Le Métier à Tisser* (1957,The Loom).The trilogy was made into a highly successful TV series called *L'Incendie* (The Fire), directed by Mustapha Badie (1927-2001).

Within the pages of Mammeri's literary texts Algerian cinema found a rich mine of images that were intact, in real colours. It also found mature dialogues that were free of exaggeration and embellishment, as well as clearly defined characters who spontaneously reflected the essential nature of Algerians at the darkest moments of their historical struggle, the struggle between those striving for freedom and a colonial power dedicated to enslavement and oppression.

Mammeri's narratives benefited immensely from his knowledge as an anthropologist who spent a lifetime tracing historical, linguistic, cultural, and symbolic developments.

When the film *L'Opium et le Bâton* was released in Algerian cinemas – more than six hundred cinemas at the time – the audiences were unprecedented. The film achieved record viewers and box office sales, something never seen before in Algerian cinemas. To this day, the film maintains a strong presence in the Algerian cinematic imagination. Following the paths of the novel, the film portrays Algeria in its mythical dimension, where the dream of freedom and justice is a byword shared by all Algerians. The film highlights the ordinary Algerian, simple in his daily life but grand in his dreams and aspirations. It is a film about the individual who lives between reality and fantasy; the individual who cannot stop bursting barriers to achieve both his individual and his collective freedom.

The novel *L'Opium et le Bâton* is viewed as a smart narrative that presents the Algerian Revolution poetically and with insight, away from stereotypes, exaggerated writing, and quixotic heroism. In the novel, opium symbolised the hollow slogans employed by the colonial power in an attempt to save itself in the last quarter of the game of history. Colonial France presented itself as the patron of justice and equality for all people living in the colony – which was consid-

Mouloud Mammeri

ered a French province – so there should be no disparities between Europeans, Amazighs, and Arabs. When propaganda failed to ease the tensions, France decided to use the "stick", which stood for crackdown, displacement, torture, and starvation of the local population.

L'Opium et le Bâton is based around a family of three siblings: Bashir Lazrak, a physician graduated from Paris University; Beleed, a French language teacher who leads a schizophrenic life as both a friend of the French and a sympathizer with the revolution; and the youngest brother, Ali, who is fully engaged in the anticolonial war as a member of the FLN, the National Liberation Front. His dream is to raise the Algerian flag in the sky over the Algerian capital Algiers. As such, the family represents Algeria during the revolution for national liberation.

The film has indeed preserved the astuteness of the novel since it offers an objective and bold view of the Algerian Revolution; the war was not between the French and the Algerians, but rather between the colonisers and the colonised – there were some locals who aligned themselves with the colonisers, and on the other hand, some French sided with the Algerian Revolution.

The film owes its success to two factors. Firstly, it selected a novel that is "intelligent", strong, and poetic – even as it addresses violence. Secondly, it brought together the best actors in the Algerian film and theatre industry of the 1960s who were themselves part and parcel of the Revolution. Most of the cast were members of the national liberation movement, actors such as Mustapha Kateb, Sid Ali Kouiret, Mahieddine Bachtarzi, Larbi Zekkal, Hassan El-Hassani, in addition to the great French actor Jean-Louis Trintignant.

Screening of the film contributed significantly to circulation of the novel while, conversely, the popularity of the novel and the name of its celebrated writer have granted the film a unique reception.

Translated by Adil Babikir

1 Abu Bishr 'amr Ibn 'uthman Sibawayh (760–796) was the celebrated grammarian, author of *Al-Kitab*, the first written grammar of the Arabic language.

LULU NORMAN

Location and characters the driving force

Les Chevaux de Dieu / Horses of God,
directed by Nabil Ayouch, adapted from the novel
Les étoiles de Sidi Moumen by Mahi Binebine
The novel's English edition, *Horses of God*, was translated from the French by Lulu Norman, (Granta &Tin House, 2013)

Nabil Ayouch's film of Mahi Binebine's *Horses of God* was shown briefly at London's Ciné Lumière in 2013 (regrettably, a UK distributor failed to pick it up for wider release), not long after the book was published in English. And – to declare an interest from the off – as the book's translator, I knew it better than most. Watching the film then, all I could see was what wasn't there, because the mind's eye will always be more persuasive than the eye.

Though they spring from the same story, the film is an entirely different creature and of course deserves consideration on its own terms. Both pose the question: how was it that a group of ordinary Moroccan boys, friends who grew up playing football together in Sidi Moumen, a shantytown on the outskirts of Casablanca, came to carry out the deadly suicide bombings in that city in 2003?

Deciding against the use of narrative voiceover (in the book, one of the bombers relates events from beyond the grave), which would equip him with all the benefits of hindsight and backstory, Ayouch nevertheless answers that question in every frame of his film. It is a confident artistic decision, which not only liberates him from the constraints of any literal rendering but lets the place and people he depicts speak for themselves. Because it is the location and the characters which are the film's – and the story's – driving force.

A scene from the film Horses of God

The film was shot on location in Sidi Moumen itself. The vast shantytown, the enormous dump that rises beside it and the wasteland where the boys play football define the characters' lives. Like the poverty they sustain, they are also a matter of fact. As such, Ayouch takes them for granted, and so do we. There is no need for signposting, characters telling us how they feel, or any heavy underlining of the harshness of a dirt-poor life: it is all around. More than anything, this approach gives a visceral sense that the boys are the products of this place.

It takes off at a furious pace and the dialogue is even faster; the stories emerge from their situation. The boys' lives are spent salvaging from the dump, scraping for a penny, playing rival teams at football, getting into fights – or off their heads – and running away from trouble at top speed. Amidst the rough and tumble we find – rather than meet –Yachine (who's named himself in homage to the great Russian goalkeeper), the film's centre, and his older brother and avenging angel Hamid who will charge anyone who threatens

A scene from the film Horses of God

him, swinging a chain. There's Nabil, the son of Tamu, the town prostitute and sometime singer; Fuad and his beautiful sister Ghizlaine. All the kids help each other out, but the closest relationship and key dynamic is between the two brothers. By returning frequently to their unchanging home-life – to their mother's complaining, their father's coughing, their annoying simpleton brother, the perennial Egyptian soap opera on the TV – a sense of suffocation builds.

This is unrelieved, even when the camera soars from action at human level to the overhead shot to reveal only miles of the same makeshift life: we race high over roofs dotted with tyres (to weigh down roofs of corrugated iron) and satellite dishes, noticing the long line and sudden turns of the cement gutter. This is a whole city of no escape, all most of its inhabitants will ever see. The perimeter wall marks the limit of their lives, the wasteland stretches to a bare, blank horizon and all the colours are neutral to dull. The use of two casts, to show the same characters first as kids and then as young men, means the story can be told chronologically, but also drives the point home: they're still scrabbling for a living, still playing football, still getting into fights, still running off – only the boys have become men.

The approach is so understated and naturalistic as to be documentary, but style is deceptive; this is far more artful (and action-packed) than reportage. A lavish wedding party – all deep velvet cushions and rich brocade in a huge marquee, bleached blonde Tamu singing

Director Nabil Ayouch

on a stage, hips gyrating, couples drinking and dancing – is cut to alternate with a scene of the boys, who have sloped off to make their own fun. As they're laughing, dancing, drinking and getting high, one of them, Nabil, passes out, and is raped while he's unconscious. Nothing is made of this, it simply happens. It's impossible to think of a Hollywood or UK/ European film that would let a rape take place entirely unremarked, with no authorial intervention or any softening of the blow, so that our shock has nowhere to go.

Yachine's big mournful eyes do a lot of the film's talking. In one scene, wheeling his cart piled with oranges down an alleyway, he mutters something about being sick of his job. But the wall, the alley's dirt path, the lines of washing and the melancholic confusion of his face have all said it before he does. Dialogue and script are not sacrosanct here; what we say is just what comes out of our mouths. Like Ken Loach, Ayouch uses many non-actors and has directed them brilliantly; their reactions are so natural and fresh I began to wonder if he had also used Loach's technique of not letting the cast know the outcome of a scene beforehand, just sketching the premise and providing a few lines, so that they improvise and react in character, to retain authenticity and surprise. Which is not to take away from the players themselves, whose emotional honesty is breathtaking and never overdone; I found Hamid and Nabil, Tamu's son, particularly affecting.

It is only when Nabil gets Yachine a job working with him in a local garage, repairing mopeds for his ogre of a boss, Ba Moussa, that we have a sense of how things might have been: there's a moment of intoxicating freedom as Yachine fixes a bike and the two of them, elated, take off for a spin. They have found a shack to move into together and Yachine's longing for Ghizlaine looks as if it might finally be reciprocated.

The show-don't-tell approach pays off again as the film shifts down a gear. When he emerges from a long stint in prison, we barely

Poster for the film The Barber of the Poor District, *directed by Mohamed Reggab in 1982*

recognise Hamid: he stands still, straight and self-possessed, wearing a clean, ironed shirt. Gone is the volatile, chain-swinging youth last seen reeling drunk in the neighbourhood bar. As the Islamists glide into the picture, the young footballers' growing interest and subsequent adherence to their doctrine has all the force of logic. Here is structure, discipline and dignity. Martial arts classes channel their energies; regular meals, washing and prayer rituals follow. They are noticed; they belong. Light floods the yard.

During the film's second act we gradually, even retrospectively, become conscious of the deep undercurrent of shame that has run through these young men's lives like that gutter through the slum, inexorably feeding into the conflagration we know is to come. Not least that of Nabil, who's been the target of abuse all his life on account of his mother's job. Life-changing decisions provoke tectonic emotional shifts, yet are all-but invisible: a kid speaks to a woman who sits waiting, a basket at her feet. Tamu stands up slowly and walks off. Nabil, looking on from behind a corner, has refused to see her; he has a different, proud future in sight. The only downside to this level of realism is that it cannot deliver the devastating punch of the book, or of a more conventional film, whose characters we have come to know intimately. Its effects are far subtler; details come back and questions stick in the mind long after it has finished.

Watching the DVD's 'Making of' section, I wasn't surprised to learn that, in the wake of the bombings in 2003, Ayouch (who lived nearby) had taken his camera and gone out into the streets to record the testimonies of victims of the blast and interview the families of the bombers. The film *Horses of God* is not the book adapted or transposed; Ayouch brings far more to this table. It's a complete reimagining, a serious, thrilling and informed piece of cinema.

Note:
Mahi Binebine's and Nabil Ayouch's responses to 16 May 2003 have not been confined to their art: in the last five years, they have established the Fondation Ali Zaoua, which opened the Stars of Sidi Moumen Cultural Centre, and that has played a huge part in reinvigorating the neighbourhood (they plan to open further centres in as many Moroccan cities as possible).
http://fondationalizaoua.org/wp/fr/
Sidi Moumen is now a thriving Moroccan suburb with a small shantytown, rather than the other way around.

HAITHAM EL-ZOBAIDI

Wanted: A women's literature that can be turned into film

The depiction of the Arab woman in Arab cinema is not much different from her reality in public life; she is marginalised and portrayed as capricious. Cinema is the visual story of the 20th century, and the 20th century is the story of the rise and fall of women in Arab cinema.

From its beginnings, those involved in Arab cinema knew the importance of women to the medium. A film would not be complete without women.

The first wave of Arab films was aristocratic in spirit. These films were meant for the aristocracy and were about the aristocracy. They were replete with women who served as decor for the hero or the heroine and who were typically elegantly dressed in evening gowns, cigarette in hand and sipping champagne. The heroine always played the role of the desired object and the rest of the female cast had no story to tell. From time to time we would find the stereotypical character of the stern, domineering mother, and that would more or less complete the presence of women in the world of the rich and wealthy.

Very quickly, however, the average moviegoer had had enough of the world of glamour in films. The film industry injected doses of poverty into their productions, with their poor characters generally living on the fringes of the lives of the rich. In a typical film from this period, a poor girl would fall madly in love with the wealthy

A poster for an Egyptian film Shaqawat Banat (Naughty Girls)

hero and then usually give him a painful lesson in morality – after he had jilted her, of course.

Next came the wave of populist films of the 1950s and '60s and these included plenty of female characters. There was the poor girl who overcomes her social condition, the loving mother and obedient wife who is always cooking for her family, the rural woman victimised by the male-dominated society of her village, et cetera.

Yes, women became more visible but only in a limited number of films, and that perhaps reflected the limited female presence in the workplace and in positions of responsibility in Arab societies.

With the end of the '60s and beginning of the 1970s, a new wave of films saw the light of day in which women were portrayed as glamorous and playful. The scenarios took place on the beaches of Alexandria or the streets of Beirut. Our heroines were beautiful and free-spirited but remained marginalised and materialistic and found no problem with being treated as objects. Films of that period were crammed with scantily clad women but were desperately short on women's issues.

Our journey through history finally reaches the gloomy days of our own time. Women have certainly been present in the films of the period that focused on the ideological, economic and political convulsions rocking Arab societies but their characters had minor roles in the changes being depicted. In fact, female roles regressed from the stereotypical roles of the popular girl or that of the showgirl. Of course, women were present in greater numbers in public life in modern Arab societies and modern Arab cinema reflected that by showing more female characters. The problem, however, is that the image of women shown reflects the regression towards religious conservatism and isolation that has afflicted Arab societies. For example, actresses who are veiled insist on wearing their veils even in scenes in which their character is having a conversation with her husband in the intimacy of their home. And viewers find that normal.

A special issue of Al Jadeed *magazine, March 2018, on Women's Cinema: The image of women in Arabic cinema*

For their part, censors

suddenly discovered that they hadn't censored kissing scenes in the films of the 1950s and '60s, so they duly cut them out from the reruns of these films on satellite channels. Yep! The female body is once again taboo in films and television programmes.

In fairness, we must point out that in some Arab countries the film industry did treat important feminist issues in the Arab world. After pressure from the then Egyptian first lady Suzanne Mubarak, a film came out in Egypt on the topic of divorce. Furthermore, angry female Arab filmmakers invaded the male-dominated film industry and gave us a few revenge films.

From time to time, a purely feminist movie, from Tunisia or Syria, hit the silver screens in the Arab world, but otherwise we can safely say that there is no Arab cinema devoted to women's issues. True feminist movies in the Arab world are no more than a handful.

Cinema is always inspired by literature, so let's ask if there is a feminist literature in the Arab world. There is, in fact, a lot of literature celebrating passion and love, but it is all written by men. A filmmaker could hardly be expected to turn that kind of literature into visual drama.

In general, men write about their own world but from time to time do turn to the world of women. They, of course, end up describing it through their eyes and not as it really is. Arab cinema has always emulated Western cinema but the problem arises that cinema in the West describes women who are completely alien to the East.

The absence of women's issues in Arab cinema will persist so long as Arab women writers themselves do not take the initiative first. It is as if Arab women writers have chosen to drop a literary veil over their cause, similar in many ways to the real veil that has become an icon of our modern times. But without a profoundly written work first, there won't be a film worth watching.

Defending women's causes falls first and foremost on female shoulders. Female writers are the most suited to write about women's reality, especially in societies that do not mind regressing to the time of harems.

Dr Haitham El-Zobaidi is an Iraqi writer based in London. He is the Executive Editor of Al Arab Publishing Group.

MAHMOUD AL-GHITANI

Fallen Angels Paradise

Egyptian film Brazilian novel

The Two Deaths of Quincas Wateryell by the Brazilian novelist Jorge Amado is an important novel that examines death as a point of view, for anyone is capable of seeing death from their own sociocultural perspective. If some characters in Amado's novel are certain that the protagonist Quincas Wateryell is dead, there are others who believe that he is still alive and is deceiving them as he has done many times before. Accordingly, most of the novel's characters treat him as though he is making a mockery of them.

The novel is based on one event: the death of Quincas Wateryell, a legendary figure for those living in the underworld of gamblers, drunkards, vagrants, thieves, murderers, pimps and prostitutes – or Joaquim Soares da Cunha, the esteemed family man, ideal employee, and affable husband devoted to his wife, who enjoys a social position envied by all in bourgeois society and who suddenly rebels against the long life he lived so earnestly to undergo a strange transformation in his lifestyle, abandoning this stable life and disappearing from it. He turns into Quincas Wateryell, the drunkard and carouser who despises his own society and loves the nightlife with its pimps, prostitutes, traffickers, and vagrants. It is around the death of this man with two contrasting personalities that Amado builds a novel that derides all established truths, turning them into relative and unreliable matters, and succeeds in ridiculing everything that goes on around us in our lives, to the point of scorning the concepts of life and death in their own right.

Poster for the film Gannat al-Shayateen – Fallen Angels Paradise

But how did the screenwriter Moustafa Zekri and director Oussama Fawzi deal with this story, the adaptation of which might have been be a risky venture, because it might not have attracted a large audience?

It is worth noting that Muostafa Zekri was keen to make some changes to the original story, firstly to suit the cinematic medium to which it was being transferred, and secondly to be suitable for Egyptian society and culture. Hence, he has made the protagonist's daughter in the film –Vanda in the novel – like her father; she carries some

Egyptian actress Lebleba

of his intellectual qualities as well as the strong desire to rebel. She even revolts against her family and scorns them, taking her father's side, even though in the novel she carries many qualities of her mother, who tends to dominate and impose her opinion. If the control of both mother and daughter in the novel is one of the reasons the protagonist abandons this life and liberates himself from them, in the film it is caused by the mother's control alone.

In the novel, the daughter and aunt leave the poor neighborhood where the father's body rests at night, because they cannot stay in such a dangerous area, leaving the uncle with the body until the morning, when the funeral will take place. The daughter does not take the body home for fear that the neighbors might notice and start gossiping. However, the uncle is tired and wants to sleep. He leaves the body with three of Quincas' friends to guard it, but they take it with them to spend the evening with it. But in the film, unlike in the novel, the daughter actually takes the body to her home, and when Quincas' three friends go to the house to see the body, they kidnap it and then think of selling it.

As a screenwriter, Mustafa Zekri has succeeded in adding some details. For instance, he has added a golden tooth to the body. One of the friends tries to steal it from its mouth by force, as "The living last longer than the dead". Another tries to sell the body to medical school students. In the novel Quincas' three friends sanctify him and cannot risk his body in such a way. Zekri has also kept the wife alive in his figuration so as to stage a conflict between her and the daughter about the father, while the novel confirms the death of the wife, and that the daughter firmly believes her father has brought them shame, in full agreement with her mother's ideas.

There may have been some details that Mustafa Zekri added to the original story to match the film's medium, and some others kept as they are in the novel, but what Zekri has been really keen to preserve – even if it spoils the significance of the tale as a whole –is the philosophy of life and death as points of view, as well as the mockery of formalities and deceptive appearances caused by sick social customs and fear of what others might say. It is this that prompts the hero to abandon falsehood for another life that might look meagre to society, despite being more honest than the one he left behind. Perhaps, however, the most important feature Zekri has preserved in his film is the profound mockery of the concepts of life and death.

The Philosophy of Life and Death

This is the major axis on which we can decipher the codes of the world that Oussama Fawzi presents to us in *Fallen Angels Paradise*. This nightmarish film provides us with a vision of something have long hoped for, but have always been unable to achieve –the boldness to face death –but the daring of Mustafa Zekri as a distinguished scenarist makes him present it to us clearly, raising many philosophical questions about the concepts of life and death, while all the names of the movie characters also raise questions about their meaning.

Tabl (Mahmoud Hemaida) is a high-pitched name for one that seems to face death in high spirits as a way of life. Nonna (Amr Waked), Boussy (Salah Fahmi), and Adel (Sari al-Nagar) are Tabl's friends; their names suggest they had a beautiful and lively childhood, despite their tough and violent stance in the face of life. We glimpse this childhood in the scene between them and Salwa (Caroline Khalil), Tabl's daughter, when they enter the villa to bid Tabl their last farewells. As soon as she opens the door for them, they come in lined up next to each other, their faces glancing down just as if they were are children in front of their mother.

If we are to address the nightmare the film presents to us, it must be divided into two main axes: death and life – that is, if we can separate the two.

Death

This is the creature that surrounds us from all sides. We sanctify and fear it, but at the same time reject it, trying to get rid of it by every means possible, by ridiculing it harshly, rejecting it, and not submitting to it. In the film we encounter Shawkia (Safwa), the night girl who befriends Tabl and his three friends. She is ashamed, made afraid even, by the sanctity of death on seeing the dead Tabl, so tries to close the opening of her shirt that had been ripped by his friends, who had wanted to bed her and engage Tabl with them. She goes to Hobba, Tabl's lover, to get her to close her shirt; Hobba sews it for her while weeping over what was full of vitality just a little while before. We infer this fear and awe from Shawkia's words to Hobba: she states that although his eyes were closed, she feels them looking in her direction. She does not mean Tabl's eyes here, of course, but rather the eyes of death, which scrutinise her with a voracity that makes her feel ashamed and afraid.

Meanwhile, we are presented with a completely different standpoint from Tabl, who faces death with scorn. His familiar phrase, which he always repeats, is "The living last longer than the dead." He faces death with that same smile that has remained on his face throughout the film, which conveys his cold, derisive attitude in the face of death.It also allows for another interpretation, the victory of life, a life represented in the smile carved on his face to remain immortal alongside him even after his death.

Although the atmosphere of death dominates events to the point of near-suffocation, it also merges powerfully with life, so that separation between life and death becomes a kind of lack of objectivity and even an incrimination. The three young men, Nonna, Adel, and Boussy, along with Shawkia, Hobba, and Tabl, are clinging to life with all their might, as they embody life in its strongest form.

Tabl, the intellectual leading a quiet social life with a respectable family and stable financial status, rejects and rebels against all of this to live in the underworld, the world of the night, of swindling, gambling, and prostitution. He does not want his monotonous life, dominated by a set of traditions, values, and ideals that feel to him like chains restricting him to the point of suffocation and death. Perhaps the scene in which Tabl's corpse is washed in his house, over his desk, is the best evidence of that. The camera's appraisal of his library is a projection of his intellect and culture. Its focus on Tabl's pictures with his daughter and family,those photographs under the glass of the desk on which Tabl is being washed, is beautiful.

We also witness a strong desire for life and attachment to it in Salwa (Caroline Khalil), Tabl's daughter, who carries much of her father's mind and philosophy. She wants to live the life of her father,

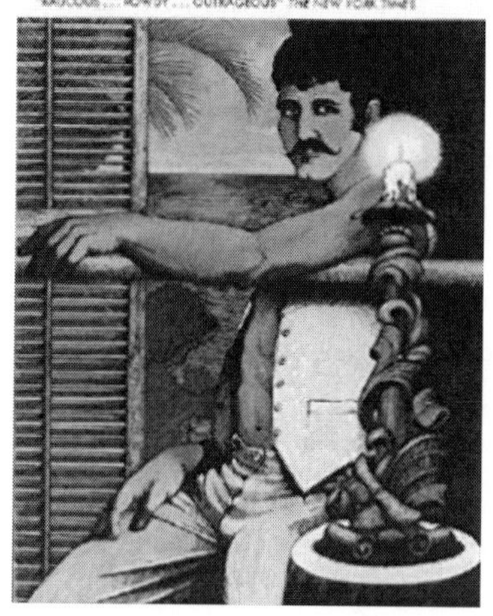

almost envies him for it, but cannot proclaim it for fear of the restrictions that bind her: the same restrictions that Tabl got rid of. She shows everyone her opposition to her father's disgraceful behavior, but in the end succumbs to sincerity. She is well aware that almost all of us want to behave like him, but do not out of fear and shame.

When discussing Oussama Fawzi's *Fallen Angels Paradise*, we cannot help but connect it to *Afarit al-Asphalt* (The Asphalt Demons), his first film. The philosophy of life and death stands strong as a bridge that connects the two films. It is life that defies death in the scene of the death of Grandfather (Mohammed Tawfiq) where Sayed (Mahmoud Hemaida) enters the kitchen lusting after Batta (Manal Afifi). He cuddles her from behind, only for her to discover that he is drunk. When she berates him, saying, the blood of his grandfather has not yet cooled, he replies, "How could I know that he was going to die today?"

Life also emerges in the scene in which Inshirah (Salwa Khattab) and Rango (Abdullah Mahmood) are alone on the roof of the house while Inshirah's grandfather is still not buried. Does this scene confront life—which is synonymous with sex – with death, or make a mockery of it?

This beautiful ridicule of the reality of death can also be seen in the scene that combines, Rango's mother (Amal Ibrahim), and Usta Abdullah (Jamil Rateb), Sayed's father, as they are reunited by the cemetery where Rango's mother goes to visit her late husband. Usta Abdullah goes there to arrange a meeting with her in the old house that was the place of their sexual encounter.

It is the mockery of death in its natural home: the cemetery.

Director Oussama Fawzi and scenarist Moustafa Zekri have succeeded in extracting the desire for life from the heart of death.

Translated by Ghada Mourad

WEN-CHIN OUYANG

Gate of the Sun

"You should have eaten the oranges"

Yousry Nasrallah's 2004 cinematic adaptation of Elias Khoury's 1998 novel, *Gate of the Sun*, begins with a cliché. The opening tracking shots follow Younes as he enters a doorway, climbs up the steps, says hello to Umm Hassan, climbs up more steps, touches two oranges hanging with leaves and branches on the wall, and meets Khalil at the top of the stairway. The camera zooms in on two oranges, now placed in the middle of a coffee table. Younes' left hand reaches into the scene, picks up one of the oranges, and his right hand, holding a knife, follows. He begins peeling the orange. He divides the peeled orange into two halves, feeds one half to Khalil, and puts the other in his own mouth. The camera dwells on Khalil's mouth, then Younes', as the two men chew greedily and with express pleasure, letting the orange juice drip down their jaws. The camera then zooms in on an abundance of peeled and half peeled oranges. In the background we hear Younes explain to Khalil that they are to eat Palestinian oranges – in fact, Palestine. The following scene appears on page 29 of the 527-page novel, in which Younes similarly visits Khalil and finds the two oranges, clearly rotten, on the wall and chastises Khalil for not eating them while they were still fresh:

from the film Gate of the Sun, *directed by Yousri Nasrallah*

"You should have eaten the oranges," you said to me.

"But Umm Hassan wouldn't let me. She said they are from our homeland."

"Umm Hassan is senile," you replied. "You should have eaten the oranges. We must eat our homeland and not let our homeland eat us. We must eat Palestinian oranges, eat Palestine and Galilee."

I realized you were right that day. The oranges had gone bad by then. You went over to the wall and took down the branch. I took the bunch from your hand but stood there confused, not knowing what to do with that bunch of rot.

"What will you do with it?"You asked.

"I will bury it." I said.

"Why bury it?"

"I won't throw it away because it is from the homeland."

You took the branch from my hand and threw it in the rubbish bin.

"Shame on you! These are old wives' tales. Instead of hanging

Film director Yousri Nasrallah

your homeland on the wall, break the wall and go free. We must eat the oranges of the whole world and not be afraid. Oranges are not our homeland. We are our homeland."

Nasrallah reverts to the symbolic association between orange and Palestine which Khoury tries to unravel. Orange has been a symbol of Palestine since Ghassan Kanafani (1936-1972) published his collection of short stories, *The Land of Sad Oranges*, in 1963. Khoury playfully unpacks this symbolism and formulates a timely reminder that Palestine cannot be reduced to a symbol and that she is embodied by the Palestinians living in exile and under occupation. Her history is necessarily the sum total of individual Palestinian stories unfolding on the global stage.

By once again reducing orange to a symbol of Palestine, and in the way he does so, Nasrallah efficiently sets up in a few minutes his four-hour and thirty-six minute film as a national epic (that on occasions lapses into the allegorical mode), and speedily articulates the central relationship between Younes and Khalil, who in both Nasrallah's film and Khoury's novel represent two generations of Palestinians. This allows the film to tell the story of Palestine from two temporal and geographical perspectives along a clear line of narrative development. Through Younes, who was born in Galilee but happened to be 'outside' fighting the British when Palestine was lost to the Israeli occupation in 1948, and Khalil, who was born in a refugee camp in Lebanon in the post-Nakba period, the stories of Palestinian exodus, their love and war in refugee camps, and their entanglement in the Lebanese civil war are visualized in vivid, colourful, graphic details. Central to both the

Elias Khoury, the author

film and novel are their respective love stories. Younes sneaks back to Palestine frequently to meet his wife Nahila in a cave known as Bab al-Shams, and Khalil forms a clandestine relationship with Shamsa, who assassinates a Palestinian militia leader and is in turn executed.

The clarity of Nasrallah's storyline comes at a cost. The sombre tone of the film suppresses the playfulness of Khoury's writing, and the linearity of the national epic subdues his hopscotch narrative mode, as well as the multiplicity of the voices and perspectives framing and informing his narrative. The incongruity between Nasrallah and Khoury's storytelling strategies points to challenges inherent in adapting novels into films. Cinema and literature work within different traditions of representation, address divergent audiences, and engage with our imaginary variously. How can a film, even in its longest form, convey a literary text that thrives on unpredictable movement from one voice to another, one temporality to another, and one location to another, without fearing that the reader will get lost? The reader can always pause, return to where he gets lost and find his way again. What of the viewer of a film? What can she do when the film unfolds before her eyes in a movie theatre, where she has no recourse to a pause or rewind button?

NAJLAA ELTOM

The Wedding of Zein

What genre could the film possibly be?

There is a golden age that is never here, never now, for things. Sudanese literature had one. It was in the 1960s and '70s, claim mainstream critics. Tayeb Salih's novella *The Wedding of Zein* (1962) was published around the beginning of that age. During those two decades Sudanese literature came under two overarching influences – a waning socialist realism and an ambivalent vanguardism that sought to rethink the traditional and the institutional. Form continued to be a major question for Sudanese writers as traditional ways of thinking were put to the test under the pressure of modernisation, internal conflicts and fluctuating ideologies. Things seemed to happen rather quickly – from the rising population to the failing Pan-Arabism project, and a formidable globalization process (served freely with the IMF's extra pain of the 1978 structural adjustment program). Stumbling through the rubble of heavy-handed postcolonialism, Sudanese literature fought to stay sober.

Romance in the time of neo-capitalism: Why genre fiction matters?

In 1976, Tayeb Salih's novella *The Wedding of Zein* was adapted into a feature film by Khalid Al Siddiq, a Kuwaiti film director. It is quite an experience to watch a film based on a book you think you don't remember very clearly. Then you realize you remember it rather too

A scene from the film The Wedding of Zein

Khalid Al Siddiq, director of the film The Wedding of Zein

well. Then you strongly disagree with the interpretation. That is good, because at least you don't get to be confused. Now, you begin to better understand the book. The moment I finished watching Khalid al Siddiq's film I asked myself: since the magic realism genre features strongly in the book, what genre could the film possibly be? I had no idea. That was something beyond the disappointment of a reader who thinks the book is way better than the movie. It was about the fundamental philosophical joy the book brings around.

For me, Salih's novella was a successful critique of what is poor and boring: socialist realism, empiricism, and power structures. It is a pure and classic romance between unlikely lovers with a happy ending, a wedding! The whole book is a long happy ending. Why did Salih opt to produce such a brave folkloric, almost naïve type of genre fiction in a time of disillusion and disbelief? The answer is its form. Writers will go after forms that allow radical statement. In this case, political resistance at the level of an individual's subjectivity together with the collective realization of a Truth, in the Badiouian

Tayeb Salih

Cover of edition by NYRB, USA, 2010

sense. The Wedding is an Event that produces individual situational truth. Magic realism can support such aspiration. It is worth mentioning that Salih's contribution to the genre is somehow overlooked. Three of his major works namely *The Wedding of Zein* (1962), *Daw al-Bayt* (*Bandershah I*) (1971), and *Maryud* (*Bandershah II*) (1976), bear vivid elements of magic realism.

Fredric Jameson reads magic realism as "a possible alternative to the narrative logic of contemporary post-modernism"*. Salih's romance proposes an alternative utopia: mysticism and philosophical laughter. The moment he was born Zein burst into laughter. It must always be read as a sign of alarm – "something is wrong", and the reader would be out of her comfort zone for the rest of the story. Zein is laughing at me, me, at what constitutes my existence, my void, my embarrassment? The film makes the audience laugh: "something is wrong and funny, I'm in control", and they are brought back to their comfort zone. The audience joins Khalid al Siddiq in his anthropological laboratory trying hard to make sense of dark insensitive thoughts about African supernatural practices. The director focuses on the local customs, gatherings, shouting, dancing, there is never a deliberately prolonged silent moment so that we can hear Zein's laughter trashing the systems of power.

In the book miracles happen, in the film they disappear. It is striking that in the book Salih makes it clear that the laughter stops when Ni'ma is around; we see it in the film too but without understanding the reason behind it. In the book Salih shows us that Ni'ma is a serious deal. She despises modern schools, and stays the avid learner that she is. She takes her fate in her own hands. Her love brings pain to Zein's soul, which is heavy, and makes Zein remember or forget something we are not in a position to know. Both characters cut through reason, hegemonic structures – and Darwin. They both bring around the possibility of a transcendental materialism, a new subjectivity, in the Zizekian sense. Why would Ni'ma, the most beautiful and intelligent woman in the village opt to marry Zein, the village idiot? Because that makes a good romance. It is all about resistance. If genre fiction gives us a way out, then genre it is.

* Jameson, Fredric, On Magic Realism In Film, *Critical Inquiry*, Vol. 12, No. 2 (Winter, 1986), pp. 301-325

Ahmed Abdel Mohsen, the Egyptian Swiss film director, with colleagues in Karmakol, Tayeb Salih's natal village, preparing for filming The Season of Migration to the North, *a Swiss production.*

INTERVIEW WITH FILM DIRECTOR DAOUD ABDEL SAYED

"Literature is a window I look out from onto worlds I don't know!"

Egyptian film director Daoud Abdel Sayed is an award-winning film director of many successful films, very well known in the Arab world. In this interview Egyptian author **Mansour Ez-Eldin** talks to him about his experience of adapting novels into films, in particular the film *Kit Kat* from the novel *Malik al-Hazeen* (*The Heron*) by Ibrahim Aslan (1935-2012) which enjoyed considerable success amongst both audiences and critics. The other film that he adapted from a literary work was *Sariq al-Farah* (Thief of Happiness), adapted from the short story of the same name by Khairy Shalaby (1938–2011).

First of all, what attracted you to the novel The Heron?

That is a hard question. The decision to adapt a novel into a film is linked to a specific moment in my own life, to the requirements of the industry, and also to a personal state of mind, as well as the availability of stars. Consequently, there is no clear-cut answer. I liked

The Heron when I read it. I saw its cinematic possibilities. Perhaps I felt that its subject concerned or touched me in some way. Sometimes personal factors are at play. Certainly, the world of the people in that popular neighbourhood, as Ibrahim Aslan presented it with his characters and their peculiarities and imperfections, was captivating for me.

When did you write the scenario? And what difficulties did you encounter concerning the production?

The scenario was ready in 1985, but the film was only realized in 1990. The difficulties I encountered during the production of this film were the result of the prevailing ideas among producers – the film industry naturally being subject to these. At that time especially, things were harder because it was a period characterized by narrow-mindedness. There were successive trends in Egyptian cinema at that time – maybe since the seventies: there was a wave of films about drugs, a wave of musicals, and so on. Also, certain controlling clichés meant that everything that didn't go along with the clichés was problematic. You know, producers prefer to have themes, etc, that are tried and tested and please the public. There was also a mis-

understanding about the film's particularities, some producers saying it was gloomy and so were apprehensive; even the censor raised objections because the hero was blind.

What is the relation between the censor and a blind character?

The whole thing is a logical contradiction. It was a backward time and the censors were lagging even further behind. I remember I said to one of the censor committee members: Do you know that Abu al-'Ala al-Ma'arri* was blind?

And they said it was "gloomy"! For me, the film could not be further from being gloomy. So, was the comedic aspect of the film not in the script in your first draft?

No, absolutely not. But there are questions I cannot really answer till now: Did the producer read the scenario I sent him? I don't know. He said he did, but did he actually read it? And if he did, what did he think? I know a producer who used to read only the dialogue. At that time, some things were logically incompatible.

When comparing the novel and the film, I was very interested to see that in the film you leave out the political dimension that is present in the novel and embodied in the bread riots of 18 and 19 January 1977. Can this be traced to aesthetic reasons or was it from fear of possible risks of censorship?

No, absolutely not the latter. It had nothing to do with censorship. Of course, the censor would have opposed the film if I had kept in that part of the novel, but my motives for omitting it had nothing to do with censorship. The question was: what was the political point of referring to those spontaneous uprisings of 1977? Is there even a political dimension? Those demonstrations are a historical

** Abu al-'Ala al-Ma'arri (973–1057 CE) was the great blind Arab philosopher, poet, and writer.*

fact, and they are mentioned in the novel only as background. They would have taken on a political dimension if more attention had been given to them and to the reasons they erupted.

It is important to look at the form and structure of the novel. *The Heron* is a vast mosaic of a tableau that ends with the January 1977 events. The novel has an extensive number of characters, and it would be hard for a film to encompass everything there is to say about all of them. The best thing to do is to choose certain characters and focus on them and their struggles. Suppose Ibrahim Aslan had not ended the novel with the bread riots of January '77, would that have affected the novel? I don't believe they are an organic part of the work. Egyptian society is made up of its people, so we can write about it whether the riots of '77 happened or not. The only difference, in this case, is that the title *The Heron* is not appropriate any more. For that reason I changed it to *Kit Kat*.

What you have done is like a cinematic rewriting of the novel, as if you are interacting intertextually with it. Are you focussing on one thing and leaving out another for aesthetic purposes, or rather because of a certain critical view? I also feel that your adaptation of the novel is close to the process of literary editing: I am talking here about the first part of the novel where many characters appear without it being clear at first sight for the reader what the relation between them is. Did you attempt to create connections that were clearer? At least, this is what I came to understand from the fact that you made Yusef al-Najar a son of Sheikh Hosny, whereas in the novel they are not related.

The process of adapting a novel into a film or play is a process of violation, in the sense that if you oblige yourself to follow the deceitful ethical objective of preserving the novel exactly as it is, you will nevertheless betray it. Adaptation, meaning transformation, is betrayal. The logic of the image is not the logic of writing. Cinema is different to literature. If I read a certain novel that I like very much, to the degree that it totally overwhelms me, I would not go near it for a film; I would not even attempt an adaptation. For example, I love Gabriel García Márquez's novel *Love in the Time of Cholera*, but the film that was based on it, is, in my opinion, unbearable, and lacks the enchantment of the novel. I could not turn such an enchanting novel into a boring film. On the contrary, it is my duty to add a new, differentlayer of magic to that of the novel.

Egyptian actor Mahmoud Abdel Aziz in a scene from the film Kit Kat

Daoud Abdel Sayed, after a moment of silence as if trying to recall something, continues:

You haven't asked me about the most important point. That is, the fundamental difference between the novel and the film. *Kit Kat* is about failure. Every character is incapable of something. The failure of Sheikh Hosny is embodied in his blindness; the old man is helpless in the face of the authorities; Fatima is helpless in the face of two things: on the one hand the marriage her family imposed on her, and on the other she is incapable of continuing her life outside the neighbourhood; the goldsmith Suleiman is incapable of satisfying his wife; and Yusuf is incapable of sleeping with Fatima. All the characters are failing.

That is the fundamental difference, and it has nothing to do with January, or February. I don't think that that was the case in the novel. Naturally, all the details are more or less taken from the novel, but there they convey a different perspective. That is what I mean by 'violation': I take something that has a certain meaning and I work with it in another way to give it a different meaning. Perhaps it is not about transforming, but about recreating.

And there we find an answer to your first question: why exactly did I choose this novel? This is how I saw Egyptian society. A society where failure is a fundamental trait. The individual is incapable of dealing with the political system, he is incapable of living happily, satisfied by seizing only fleeting moments of happiness.

Is that why you gave Sheikh Hosny the lead role at the expense ofYusuf al-Najar? Or was it because you wrote the script and in your mind a star of the calibre of Mahmoud Abdel Aziz should be the one to steer the character of Sheikh Hosny?

No, no, that's not how I work. Sheikh Hosny was actually the ideal character to convey my idea. In his case the failure is clearer and lasting. He will remain blind. In a certain way, Yusuf later overcame the incapability in his relationship with Fatima. But Hosny will remain blind, he will remain helpless.

The elements of the film resemble those of an integrated and well-tuned poem, whether we talk about characters, place, or music. Did you expect it to be such a success?

Different aspects have contributed to the success of *Kit Kat*, among which are the original text, the reconciliation between elements such as filming, setting, music, and acting, and ultimately the direction, which created the harmony between them all.

Concerning my expectations, I expect success for every work I start on, otherwise why would I get enthusiastic about it. But it is difficult to predict the particular way a work, which has special relevance to oneself, will be received. When you are writing a new novel, can you predict its success?It is difficult.

The two films you based on literary works, Thief of Happiness and Kit Kat have in common that they discuss the worlds of the marginalized, be it in the slums or in popular alleys. Is literature a lens that compels you to fall back on it in order to access worlds that are remote from your personal experience?

I understand what you mean, and you are right, but things are not as definite as that. Indeed, I don't know this world [of the marginalized], and it is difficult to write about it myself. The experience of writingthe script of *Thief of Happiness* was different to that of *Kit Kat*. Khairy Shalaby's story *Thief of Happiness* has almost no connection to the film. The story was like a key that opened a door for me, or a window, from which I could observe, and I saw into this world that I could hardly write about on my own without this key.

Translated by Marthe Nelissen

KOUTAIBA AL-JANABI TALKS ABOUT HIS NEW FILM

Stories of Passers Through

An endless journey of exile, from when I had to leave Baghdad, age 17. A visual diary, using the medium of film and photography to process my feelings and nightmares, while looking for my missing father and a homeland that was far removed by fear and wars. I saw everything through the camera's viewfinder, from the position of an outsider in strange lands and strange towns, recording my experiences over these 30 years. The endless search and restlessness, the peace-lessness, looking for other passers through, sharing my experience, escaping the propaganda machinery expressed by the images of aeroplanes and trains. We grew up surrounded by constant news about wars, announcements by political and religious leaders, from loudspeakers, on radio and television, dominating our lives, occupying our brains. Combined with

phones ringing, disrupted phone conversations, swirling, with sounds of planes and trains providing the backdrop in the clips to the characters' painful journeys. The characters in my film, in the scenes, wash into one, with the last one burying a rock, representing the political, religious and war statements, the voice of propaganda.

I shot this feature film bit by bit over 30 years, a personal journey reflecting alienation, longing, fear, escape, with an experimental approach to style and narrative.

One of the motivations for working on this film was my deep longing for my father – a father who was executed, whose body was never found or buried by the family. What effect does this have, how can one handle this? The same is still happening. There are many wars around us, raging with the same consequences that I lived through, that are reflected in this film, and that we see daily in the reports on the refugee situation.

I am a witness with my camera throughout my exile, experiencing the world through the lens, with the time lost, the days, the years, passing by. This is why I felt that I had to capture my experiences, the witnessed events and process them into one film.

The characters who appear in my films are the same throughout, they are me. In *Stories of Passers Through* I tried even more to wash these characters into one, into nobody in particular. The characters are me and I am the characters. But since they are not defined, they have no identity. Viewers will find themselves immersed and hence it will be easier to identify with characters and situations of fear, of anxiety, of uncertainty in finding their way in this mysterious world.

The same applies to the location – it are nowhere definable, it is no man's land. This results from the homeland becoming a nightmare, with the past not even featuring in my dreams.

In the end, the film is about personal experiences, events that happened to me, and thanks to the magic of cinema and photography, a re-connection between reality and image/cinema became possible. It is a form of rehabilitation.

My intention is to present this process with the help of clips from past years. The world, the situation has not changed, especially in my part of the world, but it is also becoming more and more applicable to other countries/regions.

Stories of Passers Through is the second in my trilogy of truly independent feature films, after *Leaving Baghdad* (British Independent Film Awards 2011 – winner of the Raindance Award, nominee for Cinema for Peace in Berlin, and Dubai International Film Festival). The third, an experimental feature film, *TheWoodman* is in post-production.

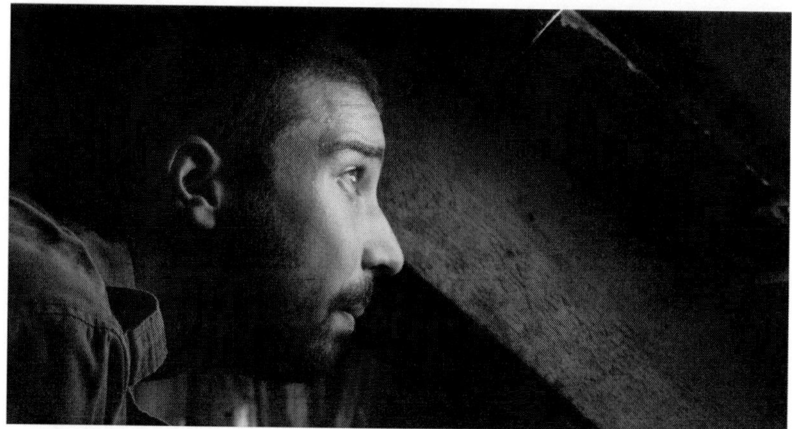

"Does an immigrant ever stop travelling? Does he ever settle down anywhere? Or does he continue to search everywhere for the lost homeland? This is the story of Koutaiba Al-Janabi, who, in his new autobiography, narrates the experiences and lives of thousands of Iraqis who have filled the corners of the earth over the past 40 years" (Dubai International Film Festival, December 2017)

With thanks to those who contributed their time and work in the realisation of this film: Odai Manea and Paul Defreitas (editors), Hanna Heffner (production), Tom Donald (music), Zhe Wu (sound), Gwynne Evans (colorist), and Nayef Rashid, Janos Szasz, Sadik Al Attar, Amer Mehdi (main cast).

All the photos are from Stories of Passers Through

BECKI MADDOCK

Men in the Sun

The harsh white heat of the desert

Ghassan Kanafani's novella *Men in the Sun (Rijaal fi al-Shams)* is an allegorical tale of exile, hope, despair and bravery. First published in Arabic in 1962 and subsequently translated into many languages, it tells of the Palestinian experience following the creation of Israel through the stories of four men. Abu Qais, Assad and Marwan are trying to get to Kuwait in the hope of finding work and improving their families' impoverished situation. They have reached Iraq and meet Abul Khaizuran, who offers (for a fee) to smuggle them across the border in the tank of the water truck he drives for a rich Kuwaiti.

Al-Makhdu'un, the film based on the novella, and variously translated as *The Dupes* or *The Deceived*, was first shown at a film festival in Syria in 1972, where it aroused controversy due to its depiction of Arabs' treatment by other Arabs and their relationships with Palestinians, in addition to its sub-text of criticising political passivity. Although the film initially received permission to be screened in Syria, this was withdrawn after a week to allow further study of the film. *Al-Makhdu'un* was directed by Egyptian Tewfik Saleh, whose films deal with social injustice, political abuse and the class struggle. It was produced by the Syrian National Film Organization and starred Mohamed Kheir Helwani, Abdel Rahman al-Rachi, Bassam Loutfi

A scene from The Dupes, *the film adaptation of Kanafani's* Men in the Sun

and Sakeh Kholoki. The film, which is by and large a faithful adaption of the novella, received the Tanit d'Or for long films at the Carthage Film Festival in 1972.

The attempt by the three men, who each represent a different generation, to reach Kuwait forms the backbone of a narrative which is peppered with reminiscences and flashbacks, relating how the hopelessness and inpoverishment of life in the refugee camps has driven these men to try to smuggle themselves into Kuwait. Kanafani tells the story of the Palestinian people through the individual back stories of the three men.

As Abu Qais repeats at several points in the story, he is an "old man". He has been driven to journey to Kuwait after "ten hungry years", during which he's done nothing but wait. He tells himself: "You have needed ten big hungry years to be convinced that you have lost your trees, your house, your youth and your whole village." After his friend returns from Kuwait with money, Abu Qais feels under pressure from his friend and his wife to travel so he can support his family.

Tewfik Saleh, director of the film

Marwan is just 16 years old. His father, in order to realise his ambition to leave the mud hut in the camp and live under a concrete roof, has divorced his mother and married Shafiqa, who no one wanted to marry after she lost a leg in the bombardment of Jaffa. Marwan's brother had been sending money from Kuwait to support his mother and siblings, but after he gets married these payments stop, leaving Marwan feeling that he must leave school and travel to Kuwait himself.

These unsignalled flashbacks make the timeline in both the film and book a little confusing, but at the same time capture well the bewilderment of one who is lost in the desert. This is particularly apparent for example when the third man, Assad, is in the office of "the fat man", a smuggler in Basra, but is at the same time recalling his experience with another smuggler who promised to transport him from Jordan to Baghdad, before taking his money and abandoning him in the desert. As the narrative relates: "His head felt muddled, with thousands of confused voices throbbing in it", and his conversation with the fat man starts to blend with his desert journey and the memory of his uncle lending him 50 dinars to travel, with the aim that he will return and marry his cousin.

The harsh white heat of the desert permeates the narrative and dominates the black and white film, as does the noise and jolting of "the lorry, a small world, black as night" as it makes its way across the empty desert. Kanafani starts several consecutive paragraphs with the lorry, emphasising the endlessness of the journey: "The huge lorry was carrying them along the road, together with their dreams, their families, their hopes and ambitions, their misery and despair ... their past and future...", and "The lorry travelled on over the burning earth, its engine roaring remorselessly."

The contrast of Palestine with the desert runs like a thread through the story, and is expressed particularly through Abu Qais, who remembers life in his village as he lies beside the Shatt al-Arab: "every-

Ghassan Kanafani, author of Men in the Sun

thing around him became simply an endless white glow. He went back, and threw himself down with his chest on the damp earth, which began to beat beneath him again, while the scent of the earth rose to his nostrils." Through this contrast, the narrative highlights the longing and nostalgia Palestinians feel for their land and their trees. "There are no trees in Kuwait, Saad said so", muses Abu Qais. "The trees exist in your head, Abu Qais, in your tired old head... Ten trees with twisted trunks that brought down olives and goodness." Buying olive trees is one of the things Abu Qais dreams of doing with the money he earns in Kuwait.

The experience of refugees at the hands of ruthless people smugglers is still relevant today. The three men's unequal power relationship with "the fat man" reflects the dishonour and humiliation felt by the disinherited Palestinians, who are trying to make something of themselves and regain their sense of honour. Abu Qais stands before the fat man "bearing on his shoulders all the humiliation and hope that an old man can carry". For Marwan, "the threads of hope that had woven fine dreams in his heart had been broken in the fat man's shop".

In contrast, Abul Khaizuran is a somewhat more sympathetic smuggler, or at least is made more human, as the author tells us something of his back story and his motivations. Abul Khaizuran has also suffered humiliation. He lost his manhood when he stepped on an Israeli mine and now cares only about money, as he repeatedly states. Despite the exaggerations and contradictions in the story he tells the other three men, as well as benefitting financially from them, Abul Khaizuran does appear to be trying to help them reach Kuwait, though ultimately he looks out for number one. Yet the Abul Khaizuran of the film, with his villainous expression and menacing laugh, appears to be more sinister than his literary counterpart. He is less remorseful, for example, at the outcome of the desert journey. In the film he appears to drive straight to the rubbish heap and dump the half-naked bodies, whereas the final chapter of the novella describes his dilemma over what to do. He feels the men deserve a proper burial, but he feels so worn out. He chances on the municipal dump, reasoning that if he leaves the bodies there they will be found and given a proper burial.

The end of the film is where it differs most from the book. In the film the men bang on the walls of the tank, whereas in the novella they suffocate in silence for fear of drawing attention to their existence. Abul Khaizuran asks: "Why didn't you knock on the sides of the tank? Why didn't you say anything? Why?" The choice to fight or to suffer in silence is a metaphor for the Palestine situation and a provocation to the Palestinian community. When the armed struggle to regain Palestine began in 1965, Men in the Sun acquired more political significance, with Palestinians taking their struggle/future into their own hands.

Ghassan Kanafani was a Palestinian writer, teacher and journalist. He was born in Acre in 1936, from where his family fled in 1948, settling finally in Damascus. He later lived and worked in Kuwait, then Beirut, where he was killed along with his niece in 1972, when his booby-trapped car exploded. A prolific writer in multiple genres including journalism, essays, theatre, novels and short stories, Kanafani contributed to many daily and weekly publications and edited several including *Al-Hurriya* and later *Al-Hadaf*, the weekly publication of the Popular Front for the Liberation of Palestine. Throughout his life he wrote in whichever medium he considered most suitable for what he wished to express.

Kanafani became a refugee aged twelve and thereafter lived in exile, not always with official permission. His life and work were inextricably linked to the Palestinian cause. Having been educated in French, Kanafani made a conscious effort to enrich his Arabic. After

A scene from The Dupes

he enrolled at Damascus University's Department of Arabic Literature, he began to write stories that realistically expressed the Palestinians' situation. His wife wrote in her memoir that: "His inspiration for writing and working unceasingly was the Palestinian Arab struggle." Kanafani was involved in the struggle for Palestinian rights throughout his life. He noted early on the contrast of camp surroundings with the longed for past and his experiences turned him political at an early age.

Kanafani's fiction lays bare the political, social and human realities of the Arab-Israeli conflict but, by concentrating on individuals' stories and experiences, he avoids theorising about the Palestinian cause. Both *Men in the Sun* and *al-Makhdu'un* are unsentimental. Through sparse dialogue and sound and stark imagery the Palestinian situation is humanised. *Men in the Sun* brought Kanfani instant and wide recognition and acclaim, and is still considered by many to be his best work.

References:
Lehman, O. Ed. 2001, *Companion Encyclopedia of Middle Eastern and North African Film*. London & New York: Routledge; Kanafani, G. 1999 (trans. Kilpatrick, H.) *Men in the Sun and Other Palestinian Stories*. London: Lynne Rienner Publishers; Kanafani, G. 2000 (trans. Barbara Harlow & Karen E. Riley) *Palestine's Children: Returning to Haifa and Other Stories*; Kanafani, G. 2013 *Rijaal fi al-Shams*. Cyprus: Dar al-Rimal; Shafik, V. 2007 (revised edition) *Arab Cinema: History and Cultural Identity*. Cairo: AUC Press

The film *In the Land of Tararanni* (1973), directed by Férid Boughedir, Hamouda Ben Halima and Hédi Ben Khalifa, was based on three stories, including "The Broken Streetlight" below, from *Saharat Minhu al-Layali* (Sleepless Nights), the posthumously published anthology of short stories by Ali Douagi. Ali Douagi is regarded as the founding father of the the Tunisian short story.

ALI DOUAGI

The Broken Streetlight

A SHORT STORY

TRANSLATED BY KAREN MCNEIL AND MILED FAIZA

-1-

A group of boys with slingshots were using the streetlight for target practice, and the cleverest of them hit it. Then the *adhan* started calling the faithful to the neighbourhood mosque for the *maghrib* prayer, and the boys scattered in all directions.

All the lights on the street were on save this one, with its broken bulb, like a bare tree in autumn. A drizzle of rain made the dark section of street even more melancholy.

There was a barber shop next to the lamp. On its sign was written in red, "Modern Cuts Barber Shop", along with the drawing of a razor, the universal symbol for a barber. Seeing the red sign, I recognised the barbering profession.

The barber came out of his shop and saw the broken light, and also that his red sign was now not visible in this section of the street. So he took the sign down and brought it inside.

He turned to the mirror to fix his black handlebar moustache, the

A scene from the film In the Land of Tararanni

kind that vulgar women of the previous century used to call a "heart-hook". He heard footsteps on the dark rainy street, and looked out as any busybody would to see who was passing by his shop and where they were going. But the darkness of the street frustrated his efforts, so he went out onto the doorstep.

Driven to investigate, he walked toward the dark streetlight and saw a woman standing there, wrapped in a white *sefsari* and sheltering under a shop canopy.

The drizzle had mussed his hair in a way that no tractor could have, and our friend was well aware of this. So he debated whether to go inside to fix his hair – which he was quite proud of and displayed as a sample of his work – or whether to go introduce himself to this woman by the streetlight, and who knows what could happen?

Perhaps he could introduce himself, and invite her into his elegant shop, filled with powder pots and enough bottles of perfume to win the heart of even the most respectable daughter of Eve. There is nothing like perfume to win a lady's heart, and then, who knows?

Finally, his ingrained habits (and I'll leave it to the reader to label the kind of man who has such habits) won over, and he went back inside his shop. He resumed his clichéd stance in front of the mirror, then started cursing his shopboy for misplacing the comb.

"That son of a bitch. If I've told him once I've told him a thousand times: put the comb on the right side. And, dammit! He goes and puts it on the left side. Whatever I tell him, he does the opposite. I think he must be left-handed and doesn't know his right from his left!"

His joke seemed to please him. So much so that he took to repeating it, loudly, hoping that the woman standing next to his shop might hear it (and, indeed, she would have had to have been deaf not to hear it). Then he laughed out loud, looking in the mirror and combing his wet hair. He lingered, gazing at his reflection, as he found it (for the millionth time) an attractive, handsome visage. Especially his black handlebar moustache.

How about going out to the woman waiting, and trying out his attractiveness on her?

So our friend went out into street and peered around with his sharp eyes (eyes that never missed a single hair), but the woman had left. His prey had escaped. So he lost his temper and took to cursing the rain, and hair, and women.

-2-

The worshippers emerged from the mosque after evening prayers, pulling their burnouses over their heads and rushing home. Seeing them pass in front of his shop, the barber was reminded that he had promised to meet his friend Ismail at Café Hajj Ali after the evening prayers. He put on his jebba and fixed his fez on his head. He turned off the light hanging from the ceiling and searched all his pockets for the key, before finally finding it in the little tin pot, where he usually kept it. He shut the door. Opened the umbrella. Was about to go. Suddenly, he turned toward the darkened streetlight, and saw the woman standing there.

He said to himself: "Is this the same woman who was there before? No. That one clearly left, since I couldn't find her when I came out the second time. But who is she, I wonder? And why is she standing by the streetlight just like the other woman was? I will go to her and find out."

He headed towards her and said: "Good evening, madam."

Tunisian writer Ali Douagi (1909–1949)

"Good evening."

"Would you like to share my umbrella? It looks like the rain has stranded you. I will take you wherever you want to go, if you just tell me your destination."

"God is my destination."

"Of course! We are all heading toward God. But you are standing under a streetlight and it's raining cats and dogs. And don't you think the night is dark and a little scary?"

"I fear none but God."

"That goes without saying! We all fear none but God . . . as well as those who don't fear God – the world is full of them."

"I can see that."

"You can see what?"

"The world is full of them. You, for instance. Why are you bothering me? How do you know me?"

"I don't know you. But we could get to know each other."

"Go away and may God guide you. Leave me be with my worries."

"Wouldn't you like me to help you with that?"

"With what?"

"With whatever's bothering you." He was encouraged by her silence and so continued: "I don't want anything, just to help you. Listen, let me cover you with my umbrella."

"All right, but only if you don't get too close. And you promise not to say a word." As she said this, she wagged at him the nicest finger he had ever seen on a woman's hand.

The barber answered her, looking at her hand, and the valuable diamond glinting in the dark. "All right, then, let's go."

-3-

Our friend, given his profession, was an expert in perfumes and colognes. But he couldn't identify this woman's perfume. So he started wondering . . . "Is it Fairville, or Nuit de Paris?" Finally he asked her: "What is the name of your perfume, please?"

"Didn't we agree, not one word?"

"But I am a barber, I just wanted to know the name."

"From every bouquet, one flower."

"Great . . . who bought it for you?"

"What?"

"I said, where did you buy it?"

"None of your business. Now be quiet, or else let me go back to where I was."

"Not another word. If someone doesn't want you to talk, it's better to keep silent. As our ancestors said, if talking is silver then silence is 'a flower from every bouquet'. It's a good name, what can I say? It smells good and I could smell it even in my shop. It beat all the scents that I have, when you were standing under the light . . . Though I still don't understand why you were standing there. Okay, I'll be quiet now."

"Yes, shut up. Good God, you're like a dog with a bone, you won't let it go."

"Take it easy, take it easy. What can I say?"

"I'm telling you to stop talking and you're asking me what can you say?"

"No, it's just because I saw you standing there. And then I looked again and couldn't find you. Then when I left to go home I saw that you were back."

"Get your hand off my shoulder!"

"Okay, okay, but I just want to know!"

"Ough!"

"Where are you going?"

"Why?"

"So I know which road to take. Sobkhat Tronja?"

"No, Sobkhat Bab al-Jazeera."

"All right, but that's in the other direction. If I had known I would have taken . . ."

"Enough, then, let's go back. If you had asked me about that first thing, we would've arrived by now."

They walked back to al-Basha Avenue again. They had only gone a few steps when the rain got stronger, so the woman pressed in closer to him and he felt her warmth. They walked together as if they were one person until they passed by the streetlight and so by his shop.

She asked him, choking on her words: "Do you have a home?"

"Do you think I sleep on the streets like a cat?"

"Could you let me spend the night at your place? Or are you married?"

"God forbid! No, I'm still single. Just me and my mother."

"I will go with you to your place, but on the condition that nobody sees me, and that you will do exactly as I tell you. Understood?"

If he had been able to see the poor woman, he would have seen a single tear, like a pearl, spilling from her eyes as she said this. But he couldn't and so answered her, laughing: "You are most welcome in my home. This is an unexpected gift!" (this was one of his choicest bits of flattery).

She was leaning on the arm of the couch and he was sitting in a chair, facing her. She asked him what time it was. When he told her it was 2 a.m., she got out a cigarette and lit it. Then she looked at her new friend and said: "You know, I am not what you think I am."

"Excuse me? Did I say anything?

"You don't need to say anything. I just wanted to tell you that I didn't come with you because I was enamoured with your eyes or your hairstyle. Rather, I did what I did to get my revenge."

At this the barber yelled, stunned: "Revenge on whom? On me??"

Glossary

adhan: the call to prayer, sung out by a muezzin from the minaret of a mosque

burnous: a long cloak of coarse woollen fabric with a hood, usually white or ivory in colour

jebba: a full-length tunic made of silk or other thin, shiny material, usually with decorative embroidery along the center of the chest

maghreb: sunset; one of the five proscribed daily prayer times in Islam

sefsari: a long, single piece of white or ivory fabric that is wrapped around the body (covering the hair but not the face) and held in place with one hand

The Broken Streetlight (in Arabic *al-Musbah al-Mudhlim*)
is translated from the collection of Ali Douagi's short stories
Saharat minhu al-Layali (Sleepless Nights)

FADHIL AL AZZAWI

The present in the past form

Iraqi poet and writer Fadhil al-Azzawi writes about how his novella *Al-Qal'a al-Khamisa* (The Fifth Castle, which was published in English under the title *Cell Block Five*) became a movie in Syria. Sonallah Ibrahim wrote the screenplay. It was directed by Bilal al-Sabouni and released in 1979.

O darkness of the prison, cover us! / We like living in darkness. / There is nothing after the night, but a dawn of glory rising up.

The film of *Cell Block Five* (1979) opens with this famous time-honoured revolutionary song, often sung in their cells by political prisoners not only in Iraq, but also in many other Arab countries. From the very beginning, the film indicates the political nature of its storyline, which is based on my novella *Al-Qal'a al-Khamisa* (*Cell Block Five*), published by the Union of Syrian Writers Press, 1972, and later translated into English by William Hutchens (AUC Press, 2006 and Arabia Books, 2008). The Egyptian writer Sonallah Ibrahim, who was imprisoned under the Nasser regime in Egypt, wrote the screenplay.

It was in fact a very daring and unprecedented move on the part of the Syrian director Bilal al-Sabouni to make a film which speaks out against the terror and torture tactics widely used against political opponents in prisons throughout the Arab world.

The story follows a young man who is mistakenly arrested in a coffee house. Although there do not appear to be any known charges

our scenes from the film

against him, he stays in prison year after year, for the police have lost his file and the reason for his imprisonment remains unidentified. In the original text, the regime and the period of time in which the events take place are not specified, affording the story a universal quality: it could happen anywhere and at any time. That said, the film was of course considered to be directed against the present regime in Syria. However, given that censorship would never have allowed the release of such a film, the screenwriter and director employed a certain strategy: they set the film in the past, under a particular politically condemned military dictatorship. But even in this past setting, it is not so difficult to see the face of the present time.

The film and the novella do undoubtedly differ. The film condemns the brutal torture and dictatorship from a revolutionary point of view. Most of its characters are militants and activists. There are only two fronts: the freedom fighters and their oppressors. Salam, one of the figures, formulates it thus: "There is a war and the only justice in the world is to win this war." Whilst this is important, it reflects merely one dimension of the original text. What I wanted to do with my story was to not only ap-

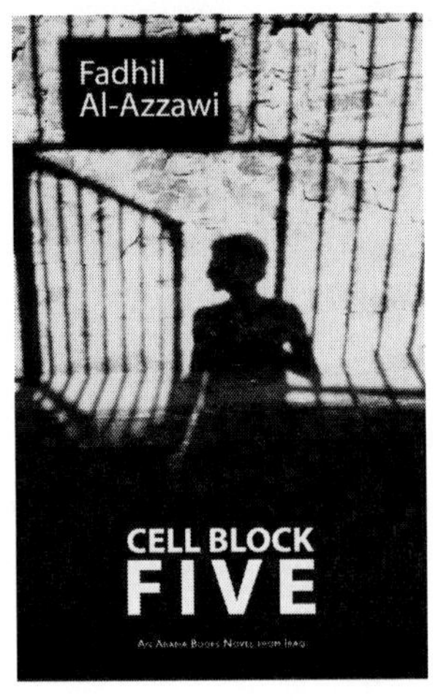

plaud the heroic spirit of the political prisoners, but also to portray them as real humans, flesh and blood, in both their strengths and their weaknesses.

There are also many philosophical aspects in the original text which are not so apparent in the film: in particular, how the victim turns into tormentor and the tormentor into victim. Salwa, who is the sister of Mun'im, one of the prisoners, and is in love with the hero of the film, represents the ideological utopia – the dream – yet this will ultimately be betrayed. Salwa will get married to a rich man and forget her incarcerated lover.

The terror in the countries under dictatorship is rather a metaphysical phenomenon. It takes on a cyclical form. The beginning repeats itself at the end; the roles alone are changed. In the opening scenes we see Salam talking to the main character of the story, who asks him innocently: "Am I going to stay here for a long time? I haven't done anything wrong. I am innocent." Salam replies: "That's not important. You are now among us, and that is all." At the end, we likewise see our young hero himself taking on Salam's old role as leader when engaging with one of the newcomers to the prison, repeating the same old answer to the same old question.

What the story and the film try to tell us is: under the dictatorship you cannot be neutral, you have only one choice – to stand against it.

And now let us consider: has the film succeeded in embodying the main ideas of the story? Yes, but only to some extent.

When I wrote *Cell Block Five*, I loved my characters because I knew them well. I knew how they talked and how they moved, but when watching the film I was unable to sympathize with them. They were somehow other people, strangers. But that is usual. When you write your story, you write it alone. In creating a movie there will be many others beside you.

At any rate, the film was a cry through the long night of Arab dictatorships, and this is no small thing for me.

LAURA FERRERI

"No more night, when the chains have broken"

The film and the book of *Al Khubz al-Hafi / For Bread Alone* by Mohamed Choukri. Film screenplay by Rachid Benhadj. Producer Roberto de Laurentis. Italian/Algerian/ French/Moroccan production, 2004. Released 2005.

"If some day the people decide to live, fate must bend to that desire. / There will be no more night when the chains have broken."

A twenty-year-old Mohamed Choukri heard these words from a poem written by Tunisian poet Abu al-Qassim al-Shabi in a Moroccan prison cell in 1952. Another inmate read them to Choukri, having written them up on the cell wall, and explained their meaning: the willpower of the people is stronger than what is imposed on them from above. It is a turbulent time in the country, Moroccans are tired of the French protectorate and are rallying for their independence. Listening to this poem Mohamed Choukri realises the power of the written word and how important it is for a person's freedom to be able to read and write. In that same cell, he writes the first "alif" (a in Arabic) of his life. From there, his thirst for knowledge will lead him to become one of the most prominent Moroccan figures in Arabic modern literature.

For Bread Alone, Choukri's autobiographical first novel, is the story of the first twenty years of his life. It is closely replicated in the film of the novel, which finished filming a few months after Mohamed Choukri died. Born in the north of Morocco, in the region called the Rif, Choukri lives in dire conditions for most of his childhood. Eight of his siblings died very young from malnutrition, only Mohamed and his younger brother, Abdelqader, are still alive when the narration begins. A terrible famine has affected the region after months of drought and most of the Riffians are moving to the city looking for food and employment. Choukri's family are among

them, travelling on foot to Tangiers, where they believe there is plenty of bread for everyone. Unfortunately, the reality of the city is very different from what they expected; food is still scarce, and Mohamed's father, a violent drunk, does very little to provide for his family. One night, in a fit of anger, Mohamed's father strangles Abdelqader, who was crying for food, in front of the powerless eyes of Mohamed and his mother. This episode changes Mohamed forever: he starts questioning his father's behaviour, hating him for killing his brother and abusing his mother. At the same time, he does not understand why his mother does not run away. He wants to protect her, but has to resign himself to the fact that she will not change her life, so he decides to escape and seek a better fortune alone.

Living on the streets, Mohamed tries to survive in any way possible, even stealing or prostituting himself, finding relief in alcohol and hashish. He grows up in an environment that does not allow him to be a child, but, in the way he looks at the world, especially at women, he shows a kind of naivety, meaning that he has not lost hope and allowed distrust and hatred to take over.

In the novel, Choukri describes the events of his childhood plainly and forcefully as they happened however shocking, harsh and violent, pulling no punches. He speaks freely of his encounters with prostitutes, his drinking, and smoking hashish, and does not feel the need to try to sanitise or conceal any aspect of his life. For this reason, the book was published first in its English translation, in 1973, and only appeared in the original Arabic in 1982, when the author paid for its publication himself. However, the Arabic edition was soon banned by many Arab governments that deemed the topics discussed unacceptable. Despite the ban, the book continued to circulate illegally and became a cult read for young Arabs, among them the Algerian director Rachid Benhadj, who first read it when he was a teenager.

Benhadj was fascinated by the universal messages of the novel. Not only the idea of refusing to surrender to the hardships of life, but most importantly the power of knowledge. Benhadj, like Choukri, had lived the first years of his life under French colonial rule, and therefore could easily relate to the struggle of the Moroccan people; and he appreciated the important role that knowledge plays in a country's struggle for independence and democracy. It felt almost natural for him – when he had the chance – to adapt the novel into a film. Benhadj also appears in the film, playing the role of the inmate who writes the poem on the cell wall and teaches Mohamed how to write the alphabet, a choice that, in my opinion, shows how important the message of the story was for the director.

Poster for the film

Watching the film completes the experience, for the non-Arab reader, of understanding Choukri's work. The film shows Choukri's story re-interpreted by a fellow Arab, who can relate to the life experience of the author more easily than people in the West, and can give it its true perspective. The director has sometimes softened athe violence of the story, leaving it to the imagination of the spectator, but never failed to show Mohamed's struggles and his dire living conditions.

Winner of a Golden Globe, the film has had the merit of extending Choukri's audience all over the world, having been shown at several festivals in Europe and even at the Cairo Film Festival, which is particularly interesting considering that the book is banned in Egypt.

Watching a film after reading the novel it orginated from often results in unfulfilled expectations. We all visualise what we are reading in a different way and it is nigh impossible for a director to create a film that suits the imaginations of all readers. In the case of For Bread Alone, however, the reader will definitely not be disappointed by the screen "version", as the director has done an amazing job of keeping the author's soul alive.

Anna Ziajka Stanton reviews

The Diaries of Waguih Ghali: An Egyptian Writer in the Swinging Sixties

Edited by May Hawas

Published by The American University in Cairo Press, Cairo, 2016–2017. Two volumes.
ISBN 9789774167805

A strangely intimate experience

Despite having published admittedly very little during his short lifetime, Waguih Ghali's is a familiar name to many readers of Arabic literature. Ghali's sole novel, *Beer in the Snooker Club* (1964) enjoyed a devoted, if cult, following for decades after his suicide in 1969, and today it is a fixture on literature syllabi at universities worldwide. Written in English and set largely in 1950s Egypt, the novel defies categorization: part coming-of-age story, part socio-historical document, and part acerbic critique of President Gamal Abdel Nasser's pugilistic and exclusionary brand of Egyptian nationalism. *Beer in the Snooker Club* was translated into Arabic in 2006 and again in 2011, and has most recently found a new audience in post-Arab Spring Egypt, where it has been hailed as a cautionary tale of the perils of military rule.

Born around 1930 into a Coptic family in Alexandria, Egypt, Ghali spoke Arabic and French at home, and later learned German, although for writing he preferred English. Ghali's diaries, newly published in two volumes by The American University in Cairo Press and edited by May Hawas, demonstrate his capacity for an English prose style that is moving, lyrical, and never less than bracingly honest. For those who have read *Beer in the Snooker Club*, Ghali's authorial voice will seem to closely resemble that of Ram, the novel's lovelorn and devastatingly self-conscious protagonist, whose carefree exis-

tence masks an abiding existential unease with his own place in the universe. Whether Ghali is complaining in his diaries about the fickle affections of a new girlfriend, calling out the hypocrisy of his well-heeled friends who refuse to lend him money but are only too happy to let him ply them with alcohol and lavish meals in his humble apartment, or bemoaning his inability to write a second novel, Ram's consciousness seems to hover behind each sentence, tempting the reader to conflate author and literary creation, diary and novel.

In a number of important ways, however, Ghali's diaries are not simply a continuation of *Beer in the Snooker Club*, augmented with a veneer of verisimilitude and grit. It is, for example, a shock to meet the real Edna, Ghali's admitted inspiration for Ram's love interest in the novel. In the diaries she appears as no more than a wealthy Jewish woman living in London whom Ghali unabashedly exploits for money and casual sex. And yet even as he distinguishes the real-life Edna from her fictional counterpart, he, too, seems taken with the fantasy that they could somehow be one and the same: "Even I have believed she existed," he writes. Moreover, whereas the novel's melancholy tone is tempered by bursts of humour and its narrative buoyed by Ram's relationships with other characters less disaffected than he is, his diaries have much fewer moderating influences. At several points Ghali descends into a depression so profound that his account threatens to collapse under the impending weight of its own inevitable denouement: the author's death by a deliberate overdose of sleeping pills, just shy of his fortieth birthday.

The published diaries reproduce the contents of six notebooks that Ghali filled between 1964 and 1968. The first volume primarily records his time living in West Germany, where he worked as a bureaucrat in an office of the British Army. The second volume picks up after he has relocated to London at the urging of his editor Diana Athill, who lodged him free of charge in her own house and to whom he entrusted his diaries after his death. Hawas' meticulous editing enables the reader to move easily through the two slim books, surely no small feat given Ghali's erratic orthography – some examples of which are preserved in the published texts – and penchant for writing in his journal while intoxicated. Formerly available only as a scanned PDF of nearly a thousand ink-stained pages of Ghali's scrawling handwriting, through a collection maintained by the Cornell University Library, the diaries now offer an invaluable resource to scholars of Arab Anglophone literature, comparatists, cultural historians, and anyone eager to learn more about this unique and hitherto enigmatic writer.

The picture of Ghali that emerges in the diaries is that of a writer who, even while suffering from crippling depression, paradoxically also found much to appreciate in the world, from the delights of a well-made salad served with Egyptian falafel and freshly roasted nuts (his favourite meal to prepare when hosting friends for dinner), to the pleasures of sexual intimacy. On the latter topic, Ghali has much to say, describing a dizzying array of encounters with several dozen women over the course of his time in West Germany and later in England. One wonders here how true to life is the charming ladies' man who exists within the pages of these volumes, as we observe Ghali manoeuvre women in and out of his life, and his bedroom, with astonishing dexterity. Might he be giving in to the all-too-human temptation to craft his own image for posterity, already conscious, as he writes, that his diaries will be destined to outlive their author?Whatever the case may be, Ghali's narrations of the elaborate processes of seduction and artifice that undergird these relationships are both comical and poignant, displaying his trademark knack for extraordinary insight, complemented by an acute sense for the absurdity of human desires, not least of all his own.

A reporting trip that Ghali takes to Israel shortly after the failed 1967 Egyptian-led Arab military action to reclaim Palestine makes for a fascinating diversion. Ghali is critical of the still-nascent Israeli state and the injustices being perpetuated against the local Palestinian population, whilst simultaneously professing himself surprised by the affinities that he observes between his native Egyptian culture and that of the Jewish settlers. The detailed portraits that he offers of the young and moneyed in post-World War II Germany and in London during the Swinging Sixties (the era of the Beatles, anti-Vietnam War demonstrations, and free love) are valuable historical archives in their own right. Ghali's keen eye never fails to register the nuance of a custom, mannerism, trend, or popular reference point.

If there is something of the truly tragic in Ghali's biography, it is that his "disease," as he calls it, manages at times to overcome even his preternatural capacity for self-awareness. Athill is perhaps the sole individual in these diaries who appears to genuinely care for him, and yet his descriptions of her can be brutally unkind. When she sneaks a glance at his diaries, a fight ensues that nearly ends their friendship. She forgives him (and eventually evens the score in her own 1986 memoir *After a Funeral*, where she portrays Ghali as a barely civilized Oriental naïf who looks "more like a goat than a gazelle"), but the reader is left questioning whether he actually deserves her good will, or indeed ours. To accompany Ghali through these final four years of his life is to recognize his depression for what it is: a condition which perhaps today could have been managed with medical intervention, but which for Ghali himself was an illness he simply could not escape, no matter how hard he fought it.

Reading another person's diaries is a strangely intimate experience, entailing a temporary setting-aside of one's own consciousness to inhabit that of a stranger. To venture inside the mind of Waguih Ghali is to feel his pain but also his joy; to indulge in the giddy pleasures of a life lived to its fullest, in spite of its brevity. This is the gift that Hawas and AUC Press offer to us here: to discover for ourselves the inner workings of a sympathetic, talented, and eminently complex man.

Peter Clark reviews

Ibn Khaldun, An Intellectual Biography

by Robert Irwin

Princeton University Press, Princeton, 2018.
ISBN 9780691174662 Hbk, 272 pp, £24.95
US$29.95. E-book: ISBN 9781400889549

Inspirational polymath in the round

A few years ago I heard Robert Irwin give a lecture in which he said, to a startled audience: "The best Arab writers are dead." Robert Irwin is completely familiar with the varied writings of classical Arabic and has written on *A Thousand and One Nights*. He is an anthologist of medieval Arabic literature and has also been an academic historian and is able to locate writings in the social and historical context. He is also an imaginative novelist. Most of these skills have been poured into this work on the fourteenth-century scholar from Tunis, whose work is more often alluded to than read.

Ibn Khaldun was a polymath and has been seen as anticipating the theories of Charles Darwin and Karl Marx, among others. He was certainly a great inspiration to Arnold Toynbee (1889–1975), but has also been an influence on the science fiction of Isaac Asimov and Frank Herbert, and the subject of one novel, *The Polymath*, by the Moroccan Bensalem Himmich. His meeting with Tamerlane in Damascus in 1400 is the theme of a play by the Syrian, Sa'dallah Wannous.

Robert Irwin takes us through the life – or what is known of it – of Ibn Khaldun, describing a fluid, political world of Mamluk Egypt, North Africa and Nasrid Andalusia. Scholars and lawyers moved easily from one area of this Islamic world to another. Ibn Khaldun was

a courtier and a lawyer and, in his middle age, withdrew to write his "universal history", *al-Muqaddima*, translated by his standard English translator as Prolegomena. He links all the writings to the circumstances of Ibn Khaldun's life and the wider political world.

Ibn Khaldun was not quite the revolutionary modern-minded thinker of his reputation. He has a pessimistic view of life, stimulated by the ruins of North Africa of a former civilisation, once powerful but by his time not even a memory. His personal beliefs were rooted in the Maliki doctrines of Islam. He had an idea that civilisation had an in-built obsolescence of four generations and that renewal came from the nomads whose lifestyle of hardship and rigour produced qualities of nobility – anticipating modern writers such as Wilfred Thesiger and Bruce Chatwin. By contrast, luxury led to weakness, decadence and disintegration.

All aspects (and myths) about Ibn Khaldun are explored, including his relationship with nomads and with Berbers, and his alleged Sufism. Robert Irwin is respectful but not overawed by his subject, and is ready to state where Ibn Khaldun simply got things wrong.

His longest chapter is about what he calls the "strange afterlife". His fame was not recognised in the Arab world in the first centuries after he died. He was however taken up by Ottoman Turks, who, anticipating their own decline from the early seventeenth century, found solace and explanations in Ibn Khaldun's ideas. Early modern western scholars of Arabic such as the Frenchman Silvestre de Sacy and the Austrian Joseph von Hammer-Purgstall, "discovered" him and the first translations into French were the usual channel of European access to his work. The twentieth century has seen more critical editions, into English by Franz Rosenthal, and into French, by Abdesselam Cheddadi. It is strange that there is not yet a critical edition in Arabic by an Arab scholar.

It appears that everyone can have his own Ibn Khaldun – Marxist, liberal, conservative, Islamist. He can be the father of sociology and the precursor of universal histories, but Robert Irwin is careful not to make too many claims. Ibn Khaldun was a highly intelligent man of his times, believing in the importance of dreams and with some "weird" ideas of science. His large literary output has perhaps allowed readers to find many messages.

Robert Irwin writes with authority, and his book is a delight to read. He is an admirable guide to other leading observers of humanity who preceded Ibn Khaldun, such as al-Mas'udi whom Ibn Khaldun admired immensely and called "the imam of the historians". Though Robert Irwin can be easily distracted by entertaining philological oddities and a good story, this just adds to the pleasure, as well as the intellectual profit, for the reader.

Clare Roberts reviews

The Baghdad Clock
by Shahad Al Rawi

Translated by Luke Leafgren

Oneworld Publications, May 2018.
ISBN: 9781786073242. Hbk, 272pp, £12.99 / US$24.99. Pbk: ISBN: 9781786073228 (May 2018) £12.99 Kindle edition £3.99.

Growing up with war, sanctions and more war

Of the six works on this year's International Prize for Arabic Fiction shortlist, one in particular has become the focus of considerable debate. Despite the fact that the original Arabic edition rapidly became a bestseller and had to be reprinted multiple times in the first months of its publication, many have been quick to dismiss Shahad Al Rawi's debut novel *The Baghdad Clock* as a teenage romance, a weak attempt at magical realism by a young female writer. This reader, however, feels that such views are for the most part unwarranted. Critics and fans in the Arab world may be vehemently divided on the novel's literary merit, but let us not ignore one fact: this is a book that is getting people reading. Luke Leafgren's welcome translation opens up the conversation to an English-speaking readership.

Shahad Al Rawi's novel describes in colourful detail the Baghdad neighbourhood in which its young protagonist grows up, in the period between the First Gulf War and the present. Unfolding under the shadow of Baghdad's iconic clock tower, this imaginative young girl – who grows up with war in her childhood, sanctions as a teenager and yet more war as a young adult – tries to come to terms

with the ways in which the outside world is changing all she knows and loves. Western sanctions seep into every aspect of daily life, increasingly taking their toll on the neighbourhood's families, as one by one they make the heart-wrenching decision to leave the country. Mysterious fortune tellers appear, warning characters about their future should they stay in Baghdad. As the neighbourhood gradually empties, and she and her best friend Nadia grow up, the protagonist carries the reader through its streets and stories in a bittersweet exercise in deliberate, painstaking recollection.

Many of the rhetorical questions posed by the young protagonist reveal her anger towards the outside world for the pain it has inflicted on her country. "What does civilisation mean when we starve children and adults and then launch missiles at them? What does it mean for humanity to progress when it keeps inventing ever more hideous paths to mutual annihilation?" she asks. Her playground is the battlefield of world powers; her words "this is how the besieged play" convey both resignation and defiance. These are not the words of a naïve young woman, and bold commentary like this reveals much more depth than is acknowledged by many of Al Rawi's critics.

It would be untrue to claim that all of the literary devices employed by Al Rawi in this novel are entirely successful. The story flows easily, but a number of plot developments and aphorisms – particularly those relating to the protagonist's romantic adventures – appear clumsy and serve as occasional stumbling blocks. Perhaps least successful, however, are Al Rawi's less than subtle allusions to other works of magical realism; references to Gabriel Garcia Marquez's *One Hundred Years of Solitude*, for example, do little to add value.

That said, it is hard not to be charmed by the sense of childlike wonder infused throughout this novel, and its many sharp observations about human nature and life in Baghdad as seen through the eyes of a young girl. The novel is a testimony to the many individuals – now scattered – who would have once made up such a neighbourhood, and their gentle acts of kindness, grace and love towards one another as recounted by this remarkably perceptive young protagonist and her friends. It offers a vivid tapestry of characters, characteristics, smells, sounds and songs, all in danger of being forgotten forever now that so many Baghdadis have settled elsewhere.

• An extract of *The Baghdad Clock* appears in *Banipal 61: A Journey in Iraqi Fiction*.

Photo by Khéridine Mabrouk

Shahad Al Rawi at the IPAF award ceremony in Abu Dhabi, April 2018.

Susannah Tarbush reviews

After Coffee

by Abdelrashid Mahmoudi

translated by Nashwa Gowanlock

Hamad bin Khalifa University Press,
Doha, Qatar, April 2018
ISBN: 9789927118302. Pbk, 360pp. £16.99.
Ebook/kindle ISBN 9789927118319. £7.01.

Medhet's journey to Vienna

This ambitious and rewarding novel depicts the first 45 years in the life of an intellectually gifted rural orphan boy, Medhat, born in around 1940 in a village in the Sharqia governorate east of the Nile Delta. Portraying Medhat in all his complexity as he struggles to find his place in the world, the novel follows his Odyssey over the years, from his village to Ismailia, Abu Kabir, Cairo and Vienna.

In middle-age Medhat is outwardly successful, a family man with dual careers as a diplomat and a novelist. And yet he remains haunted by the ghosts of his past. A major theme of the novel is the tension between his peasant background and the *bandar* – defined as "the world of civilisation and luxury". Medhat observes that although after leaving the village he moved to the *bandar* and lived in many capital cities of the world, "deep down, I am a peasant. I have the skin of a peasant, the patience of the parched land he farms, as it waits for the season of sowing."

The finely crafted narrative includes a profusion of characters and subplots alongside the main storyline, and has a vivid, filmic quality. At the same time it is deeply reflective, and rich in allusions to literature, folklore, religious texts and classics. The final section is steeped in the culture and music of Vienna.

The novel was published in Arabic in Cairo in 2013 as *Baad al-Qahwa* by Maktabat al-Dar al Arabiah lil-Kitab, an imprint of Al-Dar al-Masriah al-Lubnaniah. In 2014 it won the literature category of the Sheikh Zayed Book Award (SZBA).

The English translation of the novel was undertaken by Nashwa Gowanlock and reviewed by the author. The translation is vigorous and lively, moving between different registers; the renderings of colloquialisms are well chosen.

In addition to being a novelist, Mahmoudi is a short-story writer, poet, critic, and translator. He has a degree in philosophy from Cairo University and a PhD in Middle Eastern Studies from the University of Manchester, England, and worked for UNESCO for 20 years.

He has a particular interest in the work of the great Egyptian writer and intellectual Taha Hussein. His substantial study *Taha Hussein: From Al-Azhar to the Sorbonne* (Curzon Press, 1998) was reviewed in *Banipal 4*. There are echoes of Taha Hussein in *After Coffee*.

The novel is divided into three parts. The first, "The Wolf Slayer", recounts Medhat's early life. Its title refers to Medhat's feisty grandmother Zainab, who reputedly killed an intruding wolf with an axe. Medhat's life has an inauspicious beginning. His parents are from rival clans, his mother being one of the Qassimis, who boast of being descended from the Arabs, and his father coming from the peasant Salehis.

Marriage between the two sides is strictly taboo, but Zainab, who is a prominent Qassimi, reluctantly allows her daughter Fawziya to marry the Salehi camel driver with whom she has fallen in love.

When Fawziya gives birth, she is so horrified by the ugliness of the baby that she turns her head away. The baby does not cry and Fawziya and the midwife Na'sa assume he is dead. But Na'sa returns some time later, and manages to massage Medhat into life.

Medhat's father dies months after his birth. Fawziya "continued to feel miserable about how ugly the child was until she died when he was three years old". This early rejection must at least partly explain Medhat's lasting insecurity about his looks. After his mother's death Medhat has a series of maternal figures – firstly Zainab and then after her death Na'sa (who had been his wet nurse) and his aunt Haniya. Throughout his life he yearns for love, though he tends to idealise unattainable girls and women.

At the beginning of *After Coffee* the village is gripped by scandal after Medhat, aged five, tells his opium-addicted uncle Shabana that he saw Salama, a Qassimi, carrying a Salehi girl, Zakiya, into a cornfield. The lovers had gone separately into hiding and their whereabouts is unknown. Zakiya's brother Khalil is "broken by the weight of shame and helplessness" over what she has done. The novel recounts in detail the negotiations between the clans to resolve the situation, culminating in an agreement that Salama and Zakiya should be permitted to get married.

At the wedding celebrations Medhat meets a woman who will crucially shape his future. She is Marika, a childless Greek woman living in Ismailia with her Egyptian husband Salem. With her is Salwa, the little red-haired daughter of a friend of hers. Salwa immediately befriends Medhat, and Marika suggests to the boy that he go with them to spend "two or three weeks" in Ismailia.

In the second part of the novel, "The Lost Sheep", Marika treats Medhat as the child she had longed for. She nurtures him and keeps him in Ismailia, sending him to school. He flourishes academically and loves exploring Ismailia with its foreign quarter. He learns to speak Greek to Marika, and picks up other languages from the foreigners there. But these joys are overshadowed by his tortured relationship with Marika's husband. Salem is intensely jealous of this rough, sickly yet brilliant peasant boy to whom his wife is devoted, and he blames Medhat for the decline in Marika's sexual interest in him. He knows he will never be able to love Medhat, and on occasion hits him.

Salem finds Medhat's academic precocity unbearable and tries to forbid him from reading anything not included on the school curriculum. Medhat finds ways of circumventing this ban and is fascinated by the philosophical and religious questions arising from his wide reading.

After Mustafa al-Nahhas abrogates the Anglo-Egyptian Treaty in 1951 there are anti-British demonstrations. Medhat proudly announces that he took part in a demonstration, but Salem is furious and uses this as an excuse to banish him to the town of Abu Kabir to complete his school education. Medhat eventually goes to Cairo University to read sociology, choosing this subject after reading Ibn Khaldun's *Al-Muqaddima*.

The novel's third part, "The Sign", jolts the timeline forward a quarter of a century. Medhat is now 45 and his wife Saniya has died after years of cancer treatment. He is sharing his home with the younger of his two daughters, Karima, and with Marika, now in her seventies. He is wealthy enough to have taken early retirement, thanks to Marika's passing on to him the legacy she inherited from Salem.

To the consternation of Marika and Karima, Medhat suddenly announces he is leaving for a month's visit to Vienna. He had first lived there when he was writing his first novel, and had then spent three

A Boat to Lesbos

and other poems

by Nouri al-Jarrah

Translated by

Camilo Gómez-Rivas & Allison Blecker

A Boat to Lesbos is a powerful and compelling epic poem, written while thousands of Syrian refugees were enduring frightening journeys across the Mediterranean before arriving on the small island. Set out like a Greek tragedy, it is passionate and dramatic witness to the horrors and ravages suffered by Syrian families forced to flee their destroyed country, seen through the eye of history, the poetry of Sappho and the travels of Odysseus. Plus poems written while the poetry visited Lesbos during the refugee crisis. A Boat to Lesbos has Arabic, French and Spanish editions, as well as this English one, the poet's first collection in English translation.

Nouri al-Jarrah was born in Damascus in 1956 and is an influential poetic voice on the Arab literary scene. A Boat to Lesbos has Arabic, French and Spanish editions, and now this English one, the poet's first collection in English translation. He has 14 collections of poetry, and has founded and edited a number of Arabic literary magazines. His poetry draws on diverse cultural sources, and is marked by a special focus on mythology, folk tales and legends.

A Boat to Lesbos, and other poems: ISBN 978-0-9956369-4-1. Paperback, 120 pages, £9.99. Illustrated with 20 paintings by Syrian artist Reem Yassouf. Published by Banipal Books, 10 April 2018. www.banipal.co.uk/banipal_books/

years with his wife there when he was third secretary at the Egyptian Embassy.

During Medhat's stay in Vienna the story of what has happened to him since he graduated from Cairo University is seamlessly blended into the main storyline. Medhat's childhood friendship with Salwa had blossomed into a love affair, but when she pressed him to get engaged he abandoned her because he thought that as she had not been to university she would not fit with his plans to go to the Sorbonne.

He does not go to the Sorbonne but passes the exam for the diplomatic service. He goes to Vienna and writes his first novel, and soon regrets breaking up with Salwa. But on his return to Egypt he finds she married someone else in his absence. At the instigation of Salem he enters into an arranged marriage with Saniya, whom he does not know.

The 20-year marriage was a disaster that Medhat describes as a "life sentence". There is no sexual chemistry between him and Saniya, and she clearly suffers from mental illness. The reader may well think Medhat should have done more to try and get treatment for this instability, which began as post-natal depression.

Now revisiting Vienna after Saniya's death, Medhat reckons he was there "to eradicate the feelings of deprivation that had become ingrained in him. He must have come here in search of love and happiness." This quest leads him to make cringeworthy and humiliating advances towards several young women one of whom tells him in no uncertain terms: "Fuck off!"

He becomes acquainted there with two Muslim sisters from Bosnia, the elusive violinist Nahed and the warm, forthright divorcee Salma. He believes himself to be in love with Nahed, from a distance. His love of classical music is reborn and he decides to take piano lessons but "setting a goal of mastering music was like reaching for the stars".

As Medhat wrestles with his emotions and what to do with his life, the narrative switches from third to first person. He had earlier wondered: "Would he be able to make up for lost time and write the great novel that would propel him to the top of the literary chain?"

Is *After Coffee* perhaps that novel, written by Medhat? Its enigmatic ending keeps the reader guessing.

FICTION AND POETRY

The Occasional Virgin by Hanan al-Shaykh, translated by Catherine Cobham. Two young women looking for love in a funny and fearless romantic comedy for our multicultural age. Bloomsbury Publishing. ISBN 9781408895733. Hbk, 240pp, £16.99.

Tales of Yusuf Tadros by Adel Esmat, translated by Mandy McClure. Winner of he Naguib ahfouz Medal for Literature 2016. The novel's Coptic protagonist dreams of becoming an artist. Hoopoe Fiction (AUC Press), 2018. ISBN: 9789774168604. Pbk, 208pp.

Ascension to Death by Mamdouh Azzam, translated by Max Weiss. The Syrian author's first book in English translation, a love story set in southern Syria. Haus Publishing, UK, 2018. ISBN: 9781910376362. Pbk, 128pp, £12.99, USD16.95. Also E-Book.

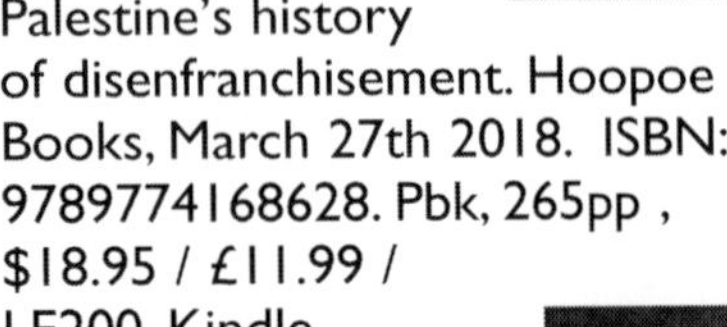

Fractured Destinies by Rabai' al-Madhoun, translated by Paul Starkey. Winner of the 2016 International Prize for Arabic Fiction. A four-part novel, echoing the four movements of a concerto, examining Palestine's history of disenfranchisement. Hoopoe Books, March 27th 2018. ISBN: 9789774168628. Pbk, 265pp , $18.95 / £11.99 / LE200. Kindle.

Night by Etel Adnan. Nightboat Books, USA.9781937658533. Pbk, 54pp, £13.00

The Apartment in Bab El-Louk, a graphic novel. Text **by Donia Maher**, and illustrations Ganzeer and Ahmed Nady. Darf Publishers, 2017. ISBN 978-1850773061 . Pbk, 82 pp, £10.99, $14.95 B61.

Withered Flowers by Stella Gitano, translated by Tony Calderbank from the original Arabic short story collection. Rafiki Print & Publishing, South Sudan, 2018. ISBN: 978-977-796-185-1. Pbk 116pp.

Hookah Nights, Tales from Cairo, by Anne-Marie Drosso. Fourteen short stories set in Egypt, from the time of Nasser to the present-day. Darf Publishers, 2018. ISBN 9781850773146. Pbk, 191pp.

Using Life by Ahmed Naji, translated by Ben Koerber. Illustrated by Ayman Al Zorkany. The dystopian novel of Cairo life that led to Naji's imprisonment for "violating public morals". Center for M E Studies, Univ Texas at Austin, 2017. ISBN 9781477314807. Pbk, 196pp. USD21.95

Closing his Eyes by Luay Hamza Abbas, translated by Yasmeen Hanoosh. ISBN 978-1291203625. Moment Digibooks Ltd. Pbk, 76pp.

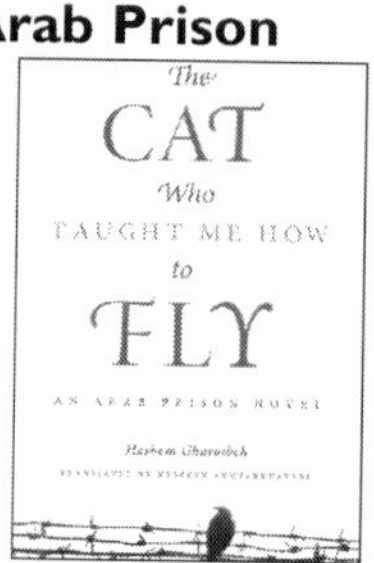

The Cat who taught me how to Fly, an Arab Prison novel by Hashem Gharaibeh, translated by Nesreen Akhtarkhavari. The story of a political prisoner during Jordan's martial law era, 1967 to 1989, and the quest for survival and the freedom of thought. Michigan State University Press, USA. ISBN 9781611862287. Pbk, 182pp, USD19.96.

Colonial Tales: The Confines of the Shadow, Volume II, by Alessandro Spina, translated from the Italian by André Naffis-Sahely. These stories, focusing on Italian military officers, are set between the late 1920s and end of World War II. Darf Publishing, UK, 2018. ISBN: 9781850772897. Pbk, 466pp. £9.99.

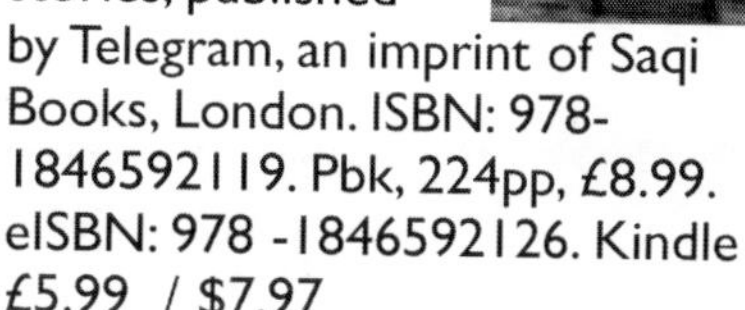

Elsewhere, Home by Leila Aboulela. A collection of short stories, published by Telegram, an imprint of Saqi Books, London. ISBN: 978-1846592119. Pbk, 224pp, £8.99. eISBN: 978 -1846592126. Kindle £5.99 / $7.97

The World According to Bahja by Rasha al-Raisi. Debut novel of Omani author. A family saga written in English by this graduate of Glasgow University. Bait al-Ghasham, Oman, 2017. ISBN 9789996920745. Pbk, 432pp.

Outclassed in Kuwait by Taleb Alrefai. The Kuwaiti author's first novel written in English includes himself as a major character. Hamad Bin Khalifa University Press, Qatar, 2018. ISBN: 9789927119385. Pbk, 146pp.

Haifa Fragments by Khulud Khamis. Debut novel on what it is to be Palestinian today, in Haifa. New Internationalist, UK. ISBN 978-1-780262598. Pbk, 190pp, £8.99. Also Kindle.

A Road to Damascus by Meedo Taha, Lebanese American filmmaker and architect. A captivating thriller. Interlink Books, 2018. IN9781623719920. Pbk, 460pp, USD20.00

Grandmother's Stories: Tales from Old Syria by Reda Al-Dabbagh, Preserving the cultural heritage of Syria through its traditional tales, White Mountain Books, Switzerland. July 2017. ISBN 978-1941634783, 210 pp,

Pearls on a Branch: Tales from the Arab World by Women collected by Najla Jraissaty Khoury (March 2018). Archipelago Press, USA.

Algaravias: Echo Chamber by Waly Salamao, a Syrian Brazilian poet. Poems translated from the Portuguese by Maryam Monalisa Gharavi. Ugly Duckling Press, USA. ISBN: 9781937027643. Pbk, 96pp.

Apple Cake and Baklava by Kathrin Rohmann, translated from the German by Ruth Ahmedzai Kemp, with illustrations by Franziska Harvey. A first children's novel for both the author and the publisher. Darf Publishing, UK, 2018. ISBN 9781850773191. Pbk, 160pp.

NON--FICTION

The Influence Peddlers by Hédi Kaddour, translated by Teresa Lavender Fagan. Kaddour's best-selling novel of French colonial rule and its persisting legacy of human chaos and cultural tragedy. Yale University Press. ISBN 9780300222883. Pbk, 344pp, USD18.00

Emirates Diaries, from Sheikhs to Shakespeare by Peter Clark. Daily life 1988–1992 when the author was head of the British Council in UAE. Medina Publishing, UK, 2018. Pbk, 272pp.

The Qur'an and Modern Arabic Literary Criticism, from Taha to Nasr by Mohammad Salama. Focuses on Qur'anic and literary scholarship in twentieth-century Egypt from Taha Husayn to Nasr Hamid Abu Zayd, Bloomsbury Academic, 2018. ISBN 9781474254267. Hbk, 176pp. USD114.00. Also PDF & E-Book.

Pay No Heed to the Rockets: Palestine in the present tense by Marcello di Cinto. Canadian author di Cinto's fifth book takes him into Palestine to meet authors. Saqi Books, 2018. ISBN: 9780863569807, Pbk, 220pp. eBook: ISBN 9780863569852.

Migrant Brothers, a Poet's Declaration of Human Dignity, by Patrick Chamoiseau, translated from the French by Matthew Amos and Fredrik Rönnbäck. Chamoiseau asserts the necessity to understand one another as part of one human community, regardless of national origin. Yale University Press, 2018. ISBN 9780300232943. Pbk, 144pp.

Byzantium, A Turkey Travelogue by Charu Nivedita. Translated from the Tamil by Aswini Kumar. Zero Degree Publishing. ISBN 9788193528327.

Khalil Sweileh, Hessa Al Muhairi, Mohammad Mishbal, Néji Elounelli, Mohamed Khalifa Al Mubarak, Sheikh Mansour bin Zayed Al Nahyan, Jack Lang, Ali Bin Tamim, Hassan Yaghi, Ahmad Al Qarmalawi and Dag Nikolaus Hasse

Sheikh Zayed Book Award 2018

The Award Ceremony for 2017-2018 took place on 30 April this year at the arts and cultural centre, Manarat Al Saadiyyat, on Saadiyyat Island, Abu Dhabi. Dr Ali Bin Tamim, Secretary-General of the Sheikh Zayed Book Award, said, in announcing the year's awards: "The nominations went through a rigorous assessment, leading to a selection of the best works from all those received this year. This was followed by a series of evaluations by qualified judging panels over a period of three months, which were brought to a conclusion with reviews by

Ali Bin Tamim

the Scientific Committee, before the final sign-off by the Award's Board of Trustees and the announcement of the winning titles of this 12th session." He added: "Throughout the past twelve years, since its inception, the Award has won a reputation for recognizing and celebrating the best texts in Arabic literary production, with a deeply-rooted transparency inscribed at a regional and an international level." The Sheikh Zayed Book Award's first year was in 2007: its aim to promote scholarship and creativity in Arab culture. The winners also receive a certificate of merit and a Gold Medal. This year the Board of Trustees withheld the award category of "Contribution to the Development of Nations".

Literature Award

The Literature Award went to Syrian novelist Khalil Sweileh for his novel *Ikhtibar al-Nadam* (Remorse Test) published by Nofal-Hachette Antoine, Beirut (2017). The novel is an insider's view of the tragedy of the Syrian civil war, with the author taking the reader around Damascus, down memory lanes, and through the psychological damage wrought by such shattered reality of place and society. It marks an important addition to Syrian literature, with its unique use of narrative tools and language.

Children's Literature Award

Emirati author Hessa Al Muhairi was the winner of the Children's Literature Award for her story *Al-Dinoraf* (The Dinoraf), published by Al Hudhud Publishing and Distribution, UAE (2017). Her story is set in the animal kingdom, where a dinosaur is on a mission to find his parallel among the other animals. Throughout his journey, he learns the differences between them, which fact finally leads him to find his connection with the giraffe, and, in a unique portrayal of the contemporary issue of peaceful coexistence and mutual tolerance of cultural differences within global society he becomes "the Dinoraf". The story is well written in a beautiful and carefully crafted language.

Young Author Award

Egyptian writer Ahmad Al Qarmalawi won Young Author Award for his novel *Amtar Sayfiyyah* (Summer Rains), published by Maktabat al-Dar al-Arabiyah lil-Kitab, Cairo (2017). The novel, which showed an extensive knowledge of music, tackles the interrelation between music and the soul, and the sublimity of the spirit versus covetousness.

Translation Award

Néji Elounelli from Tunisia won the Translation Award for *Natharayya Astiteeqyya*, published by Al-Jamal Publications, Beirut 2017, his Arabic translation of the posthumously published *Ästhetische Theorie*, the magnus opus of German philosopher Theodor W. Adorno. This work is considered by many to be among the most important philosophical

The Cultural Personality of the Year award went to the Paris-based Institut du Monde Arabe for its work in promoting Arab-European cultural relations. Sheikh Mansour presented the award to the institute's president, former French Minister of Culture Jack Lang, who said: "Culture is the most important bridge between different countries and its citizens. The UAE and France are a good example of how strong cultural relations can greatly enhance the friendship between two countries."

works on aesthetics, analysing the theoretical paradigm of aesthetics through concepts of the sublime, the ugly and the beautiful and human experience.

Literary and Art Criticism Award

The Literary and Art Criticism Award went to Moroccan academic Mohammad Mishbal, for his work *Fi Balaghat Al Hajjaj: Nahwa balagha hajjajiyyah litahleel al khitab* (The Rhetoric of Al Hajjaj: Towards a rhetoric inspired by Al Hajjaj in analyzing discourse), published by Kunouz Al Ma'refa Publishers, Amman (2017). The book elaborates Al Hajjaj's connections to rhetoric and discourse, analyzing clearly and eruditely foundational strategies through ancient to present-day rhetoric, with an extensive bibliography.

Arab Culture in Other Languages Award

The Arab Culture in Other Languages Award went to German researcher Dag Nikolaus Hasse for his work *Success and Suppression: Arabic Sciences and Philosophy in the Renaissance*, published by Harvard University Press, 2017. The book is a significant work of scholarship that fills an important gap in modern knowledge: detailing how works of Arabic sciences and philosophy influenced the intellectual development, debates and controversies of the Renaissance.

Publishing and Technology Award

Dar Al-Tanweer (Beirut/Cairo/Tunis) won the Publishing and Technology Award. The publishing house is seen as an influential press that contributes generously to spreading Arab culture, encouraging both authorship and translation. It also takes a leading role in bringing forward the young voices in philosophy and literature.

Ibrahim Nasrallah wins 2018 International Prize for Arabic Fiction

Dima Wannous, Amir Tag Elsir, Ibrahim Nasrallah

Harb el-Kalb al-Thaniya (The Second War of the Dog) by Ibrahim Nasrallah was, Tuesday 24 April 2018, announced as the winner of the International Prize for Arabic Fiction.

Walid Shurafa, Aziz Mohammed, Shahad Al Rawi

The Second War of the Dog, published by Arab Scientific Publishers, was named as this year's winner by Chair of Judges Ibrahim Al Saafin at a ceremony in Abu Dhabi. Al Saafin declared: "*The Second War of the Dog* is a masterful vision of a dystopian future in a nameless country, using fantasy and science fiction techniques. With humour and insight, it exposes the tendency towards brutality inherent in society, imagining a time where human and moral values have been discarded and anything is permissible, even the buying and selling of human souls.

"The novel focuses on the corrupt main character, Rashid, who changes from an opponent of the regime to a materialistic and unscrupulous extremist. Nasrallah reveals the intrinsic savagery in human beings, as he describes a futuristic world where greed intensifies and human values and ethics are ignored."

Professor Yasir Suleiman, chair of the board of IPAF trustees, commented: "Ibrahim Nasrallah's novel paints a chilling picture of humanity in all its destructive potential. Without a moral compass, the protagonist lets go of the normal bounds that constrain human behaviour. Nasrallah expertly draws the reader into this world from different vantage points, using crisp language in which humour makes the moral burden of relating to the main character 'bearable', or just so. His win is an accolade well deserved."

The Second War of the Dog was chosen by the IPAF judges as the best work of fiction published between July 2016 and June 2017 from 124 entries from 14 countries. On the 2018 judging panel with chair Ibrahim Al Saafin, a Jordanian academic, critic, poet, novelist and playwright, were: Inam Bioud, an Algerian academic, translator, novelist and poet; Jamal Mahjoub, a Sudanese-English writer and novelist; Mahmoud Shukair, a Palestinian short story writer and novelist; and Barbara Skubic, a Slovenian writer and translator.

Al Saafin had announced the 2018 shortlist at a press conference in February, saying: "The six novels on the shortlist delighted the judges with their fresh exploration of social, political and existentialist themes. Narrative techniques were varied, from the form of diary entries and a novel within a novel, to several authors taking inspiration from the fantasy genre. They allude to the challenging new

Ibrahim Nasrallah, mobbed by well-wishers and photographers after the announcement

realities of the Arab world, from Syria to Sudan, but transcend the factual and prosaic.

"This year's six novels, selected from the longlist of 16, and published between July 2016 and June 2017, display the best of contemporary Arabic literature. *Flowers in Flames* tells the story of women in Sudan who have become objects of pleasure under the rule of an extremist group, and in *Baghdad Clock*, a young Iraqi girl and her best friend watch their lives change beyond recognition in war-torn Baghdad. Meanwhile, *Heir of the Tombstones* focuses on an Israeli artists' village to explore the plight of the Palestinian people. *The Critical Case of 'K'* takes the form of a diary of a frustrated writer inspired by Kafka, who finds out he has cancer, while *The Frightened Ones* features a novel about a woman dominated by fear, reflecting the mindset of its narrator. Finally, *The Second War of the Dog* is set in a future world to chart the transformation and corruption of a society driven by greed."

For more information go to www.arabicfiction.org

Iraqi novel shortlisted for Man Booker International 2018

Since its announcement on the longlist of the Man Booker International 2018, literary circles predicted that the novel *Frankenstein in Baghdad*, by Iraqi author Ahmed Saadawi, would be one of the six books shortlisted, and so it was.

Commenting on the shortlist, the judges said: "This is a book that accrues in horrors as you move through it, having started very quietly with a portrait of an old woman who mourns her missing son and is certain he is going to come back. So you have this profound emotional contact with the fact of death and disappearance, and what that does to people.

"And then this entire city, with its many distinct neighbourhoods, bursts into horror with the bombings and awfulness of war. Saadawi manages to do this and at the same time to give us an overarching sense of irony – how do you get through this? How do people survive? How do they make do? What is this whole horrific process about and where does it take you in the depth of extreme?"

Frankenstein in Baghdad was published in Arabic in 2012 and won the International Prize for Arabic Fiction in 2014. An excerpt of the novel appeared in

Jonathan Wright and Ahmed Saadawi

Arabic cover of Frankenstein in Baghdad *published by Manshurat al-Jamal*

Olga Tokarczuk (Poland), Ahmed Saadawi and Antonio Muñoz Molina (Spain)

the Beirut39 anthology of the 39 best young Arab authors, edited by Banipal editor Samuel Shimon and published by Bloomsbury in UK and USA in 2010.

Frankenstein in Baghdad was translated into English by Jonathan Wright, and published in the UK by Oneworld, and in USA by Penguin. A brief synopsis of the novel, describes how, "from the rubble-strewn streets of US-occupied Baghdad, the junk dealer Hadi collects human body parts and stitches them together to create a corpse. His goal, he claims, is for the government to recognise the parts as people and give them a proper burial. But when the corpse goes missing, a wave of eerie murders sweeps the city, and reports stream in of a horrendous-looking criminal who, though shot, cannot be killed. Hadi soon realizes he has created a monster, one that needs human flesh to survive – first from the guilty, and then from anyone who crosses his path. As the violence escalates and Hadi's acquaintances – a journalist, a government worker and a lonely old woman – become involved, the 'Whatsitsname' and the havoc it wreaks assume a magnitude far greater than anyone could have imagined."

At the gala dinner award ceremony on 22 May 2018 the judges announced that the winner for 2018 was Polish author Olga Tokarczuk's novel *Flights*, translated by Jennifer Croft and published by Fitzcarraldo Editions.

Towards a New Divan:
A Celebration of East and West through Music and Poetry

A celebratory concert of music and poetry took place on 20 June at the historic Wilton's Music Hall in East London. The launch of the Gingko Library's cultural project *A New Divan* with the London-based fusion music ensemble Tafahum included the première of Tafahum's composition inspired by a new poem of Adonis, "Letter to Goethe", which had been written especially for the *Divan*.

The publication of *A New Divan*, a unique multi-lingual anthology, will be a mirror to the 200th anniversary of Johann Wolfgang von Goethe's *West-Eastern Divan* (1819), bringing together twenty-four leading poets – twelve from the "East" and twelve from the "West' – in a lyrical conversation inspired by the culture of the Other. These poets seek to continue the dialogue which Goethe started with

(l to r): Editor Bill Swainson, GIngko founder & CEO Barbara Schwepke and Prof. Mena Mark Hanna, Dean of the Barenboim-Said Akademie in Berlin

Hafiz, the fourteenth-century Persian poet whom he thought of as his "twin", the results of which he published in the *West-Eastern Divan*.

The editor of *A New Divan*, Bill Swainson, announcing the project, said: "The aim of *A New Divan* is both to pay homage to a great European poet, and, taking a leaf out of his book, to celebrate an understanding of our common humanity and to encourage engagement with the 'Other'. Of the 24 original poets – the 12 from the 'East' write in Arabic, Persian and Turkish, while the 12 from the 'West' write in English, French, German, Italian, Portuguese, Russian, Slovenian and Spanish. Our aim has been to find poets willing to engage with Goethe's ambition for his original *Divan*, but also with an awareness of the critical times we live in. It would have been possible to go only to poets already interested in 'East' and 'West', but what we really wanted to do was to encourage poets established in their own cultures to engage with poetry and culture not their own, to open themselves up to new influences and new experiences." He added: "The twenty-two English-language poets, who will render the work of the twenty-four original poets writing in twelve different languages, demonstrate the scope and quality of this hugely ambitious project."

The book will certainly create a life-enhancing dialogue in the spirit of Goethe's original. In summer 2019, many of the contributing poets will tour the UK at the Hay and Shubbak festivals, and all poets, translators and musicians will come together in Berlin, at a festival of music and poetry hosted by the Barenboim-Said Akademie.

The poets and translators are as follows:

Eastern Poets	**English Language Poets**
Abbas Baydoun (Lebanon)	Bill Manhire
Adonis (Syria)	Khaled Mattawa
Fadhil Al-Azzawi (Iraq)	Jorie Graham
Amjad Nasser (Jordan)	Fady Joudah
Fatèmeh Shams (Iran)	Dick Davis
Gonca Özmen (Turkey)	Jo Shapcott
Hafez Mousavi (Iran)	Daisy Fried
Iman Mersal (Egypt)	Elaine Feinstein
Mohammed Bennis (Morocco)	Sinead Morrissey
Mourid Barghouti (Palestine)	George Szirtes
Nujoom Al-Ghanem (UAE)	Doireann Ní Ghríofa
Reza Mohammedi (Afghanistan)	Nick Laird

Western Poets	**English-Language Poets**
Antonella Anedda (Italy)	Jamie McKendrick
Homero Aridjis (Mexico)	Kathleen Jamie
Angélica Freitas (Brazil)	Tara Bergin
Durs Grünbein (Germany)	Matthew Sweeney
Clara Janés (Spain)	Lavinia Greenlaw
Jaan Kaplinski (Estonia)	Sasha Dugdale
Khaled Mattawa (USA)	-
Gilles Ortlieb (France)	Sean O'Brien
Don Paterson (UK)	-
Raoul Schrott (Austria)	Paul Farley
Aleš Šteger (Slovenia)	Brian Henry
Jan Wagner (Germany)	Robin Robertson

The 20 June concert, including Tafahum's new composition, were made possible with support from Amal, a Said Foundation project. For all information about the Gingko Library's *New Divan* project, go to: www.gingko.org.uk/new-divan

Fadhil al-Azzawi was born in Kirkuk, northern Iraq, in 1940. He left Iraq in 1977 and settled in Germany. He has been writing and publishing his poetry since the 1960s, and has numerous collections, plus six novels, a book of short stories, works of criticism and many translations from English and German into Arabic. Two of his novels have English editions, *Cell Block Five* and *Last of the Angels*. He is a contributing editor of *Banipal*.

Liana Badr is a Palestinian novelist, and short story writer, also a journalist, poet and cinema director. Born in 1950 in Jerusalem, she was raised in Jericho, studied at the University of Jordan, and graduated from the Beirut Arab University In 1979 she published her first novel *A compass for the sunflower* (English translation Women's Press, 1989). Since then, she has published five novels, including *A Balcony over the Fakihani*, translated by Peter Clark and *The Eye of the Mirror*, translated by Samira Kawar, four collections of short stories, two poetry collections and four books of essays.

Adil Babikir is a Sudanese translator into and out of English & Arabic, living now in Abu Dhabi. He has translated *Mansi: a Rare Man in his Own Way* by Tayeb Salih and two novels by Abdelaziz Baraka Sakin. Other translations include two anthologies – of poetry and short stories.

Azouz Begag was born in Lyon, France in 1957 into an Algerian family. He is a French writer, politician and researcher in economics and sociology. He was the delegate minister for equal opportunities in the French government 2005-2007. He has written 20 literary works for adults and children. His best-known books are his autobiographical novel *Le Gone du Chaâba* (1986), which was made into a film of the same name, and *The Sheep in the Bathtub*, an account of his two years as minister.

Peter Bush is an award-winning literary translator from Spanish, Catalan, Portuguese and French. His recent translations into English are Joan Sale's *Winds of the Night* and Prudenci Bertrana's *Josafat* from Catalan and Jorge Carrión's *Bookshops* and Carmen Boullosa's *Before* from Spanish.

Georgia de Chamberet is an editor and translator with thirty years of experience in independent publishing. She founded BookBlast® Ltd in 1997 and is a founder-member of English PEN's Writers in Translation committee. She is a judge on the 2018 Saif Ghobash Banipal Prize for Arabic Literary Translation.

Peter Clark is a writer, translator and cultural consultant. He worked for the British Council for over 30 years, and has written up two volumes of diaries of his time in Syria and the UAE. He is a contributing editor of *Banipal*.

Raphael Cohen is a translator based in Cairo and a contributing editor of Banipal. His recent Arabic fiction translations include Mona Prince's *So You May See* (2011) & Status: Emo by *Eslam Mosbah*. He is a contributing editor of *Banipal*.

Ali Douagi (1909-1949) is regarded as founding father of the Tunisian short story. He wrote umpteen stories, plays, poems and songs, his short stories being posthumously collected and published in 1969 in a volume entitled *Sleepless Nights*. More about him in *Banipal 39 – Modern Tunisian Literature*, pp46-47.

Lutfiya al-Dulaimi was born in Diyala, Iraq. She has published ten books of fiction, five plays and three books of essays. She has translated four books from English into Arabic. She presently lives in Jordan. See back issues *Banipal 19* and *Banipal 30* for more of her works in translation.

Ali Abdulameer Ejam is an Iraqi journalist, critic, TV presenter and writer.

Mansoura Ez-Eldin is an Egyptian author and journalist, working at *Akhbar al-Adab* weekly. Her debut novel *Maryam's Maze* has an English edition, and her second novel, *Beyond Paradise,* shortlisted for the 2010 IPAF Prize has Italian and German editions. She has two further novels (2013 and 2014) and a collection of short stories (2017).

Najlaa Eltom is a Sudanese writer and translator. Her writing includes poetry, short story, literary essay and commentary, with some translated into English and Swedish. She contributed to the translation of several Sudanese literary texts into English, including the winner of the Caine Prize, 2017. She moved to Sweden in 2012.

Ahmad Ali El Zein is a Lebanese playwright and novelist, who is a presenter for Al-Arabiyya TV's Rowafid [Profiles] programme, interviewing cultural and artistic celebrities.

Joseph Fahim is an Egyptian film critic and programmer. He is a member of Berlin Critics' Week and the Arab representative of Karlovy Vary Film Festival. He is a former director of programming of the Cairo International Film Festival. He co-authored various books on Arab cinema and has contributed to numerous publications in the Middle East, including *Al-Monitor, Al Jazeera, Visions, Egypt Independent* and *The National* (UAE), along with international film publications such as *Vérité.*

Miled Faiza published his first collection of poetry in 2004, Remains of a House We Once Entered. A writer of political articles and literary criticism as well as poetry, he translates American poetry into Arabic and teaches Arabic at the University of Virginia.

Laura Ferreri has a BA in interpreting and translation (Trieste University, Italy) and an MA in Arabic Translation (Edinburgh University). She is a regular *book* reviewer.

Mahmoud al-Ghitani is an Egyptian write and journalist, living in Cairo.

Nashwa Gowanlock is a journalist and translator, based in the UK. She was one of the first translators to be mentored in the British Centre for Literary Translation Emerging Translator mentoring scheme. Her translations include *After Coffee* by Abdelrashid Mahmoudi and *The Crossing* by Samar Yazbek, co-translated with Ruth Ahmedzai Kemp.

Becki Maddock is a translator and researcher living in London. She translates from Arabic, Persian and Spanish into English. She has a first class BA in Arabic and Spanish (Exeter University) and an MA in Near and Middle Eastern Studies from SOAS, University of London. She is taking Kurdish language classes, also at SOAS.

Abdelrashid Mahmoudi is an Egyptian short-story writer, poet, critic, translator, who worked for UNESCO for 20 years. He has a highly regarded book on Taha Hussein, and in 2014 won the Sheikh Zayed Book Award for his novel After *Coffee.* See above p196.

Karen McNeil is an Arabic-to-English translator, with an MA in Arabic from Georgetown University, USA, with a specialty in Tunisian Arabic and Arabic linguistics.

Ghada Mourad is a Research Associate in Comparative Literature at the University of California, Irvine. She translates from Arabic and French into English.

Marthe Nelissen is pursuing a Masters degree in Arabic Literature at SOAS, London.

Lulu Norman is a British writer, translator and editor, living in London. She has translated works by Albert Cossery, Mahmoud Darwish, Tahar Ben Jelloun and the songs of Serge Gainsbourg. She has also written for national newspapers, the *London Review of Books* and other literary journals. Her translation of Mahi Binebine's *Welcome to Paradise* (Granta, 2003) was shortlisted for the Independent Foreign Fiction Prize. She was awarded an English PEN Award for outstanding writing in translation for her translation of Binebine's *Horses of God.*

Wen-chin Ouyang is Professor of Arabic Literature at SOAS, University of London. Born in Taiwan and raised in Libya, she completed her BA in Arabic at Tripoli University and PhD in Middle Eastern Studies at Columbia University in New York City. She is the author of several academic volumes and has published widely on *One Thousand and One Nights*. She was a member of the judging panel for the Man Booker International Prize 2013-15, and a judge on the 2017 Saif Ghobash Banipal Prize for Arabic Literary Translation.

Clare Roberts has a BA in Arabic and Islamic Studies from Oxford University, and an MA in Arabic Poetry and Turkish Politics from SOAS, Londo). She works at Gingko Library and is a contributing editor of *Banipal* and a regular reviewer.

Nancy Roberts is a translator of contemporary Arabic fiction, including works by salwa Bakr, Mohamed El-Bisatie, Hala El-Badry, Ezzat el Kamhawi, Laila Aljohani, Ahlem Mosteghanemi, two novels by Ibrahim Nasrallah and four by Syrian author Ghada Samman.

Anna Ziajka Stanton is Assistant Professor of Comparative Literature at the Pennsylvania State University. Her interests include the translation of Arabic literature into English (both theory and practice); the evolution of the Arabic literary canon and questions of fiction and readership in the Arab world from the Nahdah to the present; and Arabic literary prizes and book fairs. She is assistant editor of the *Journal of Arabic Literature*.

Susannah Tarbush is a freelance journalist specialising in cultural affairs in the Middle East. She writes the Tanjara blog, and is a consulting editor of *Banipal* and regular reviewer.

Yahya Wagdi was born in Cairo in January 1980. He has published his works in Egyptian and other Arab newspapers. He is the editor of the website Mantaqati (My Area) and is interested in the urban heritage of Cairo.

Abdo Wazen is a Lebanese poet, translator and author. He is cultural editor of the international daily *Al-Hayat* newspaper, based in Beirut.

Jonathan Wright is an award-winning translator whose translations include three IPAF winners, Ahmed Saadawi's *Frankenstein in Baghdad* (IPAF 2014), Saud Alsanousi's *The Bamboo Stalk* (IPAF 2013) for which he won for the 2016 Saif Ghobash Banipal Prize), and Youssef Ziedan's *Azazeel* (IPAF 2009) which was joint winner of the 2013 Saif Ghobash Banipal Prize). His translation of Hassan Blasim's *The Iraqi Christ* won the 2014 Independent Foreign Fiction Prize.

Frank Wynne is an award-winning literary translator from French and Spanish. Born in Ireland, he moved to France in 1984 where he discovered a passion for language. His translations include works, among others, by Michel Houellebecq, Frédéric Beigbeder, Ahmadou Kourouma, Boualem Sansal, Amin Zaoui, Claude Lanzmann, Tómas Eloy Martínez and Almudena Grandes. He is an honorary member of the Irish Translators and Interpreters Association.

Amin Zaoui is a novelist, born in 1956 in Bab el-Assa, Algeria, and writes in Arabic and French. He teaches literature at the University of Algiers and is a former director of the National Library in Algiers. He has six novels, with one in English translation, *Banquet of Lies* (Frank Wynne). See *Banipals 54* and *56* for more.

For more information on all the authors in *Banipal 62* and all the translators, writers and book reviewers, please go to:
www.banipal.co.uk/contributors/